Also by Barbara Lee

The Woman's Guide to the Stock Market

Take Control
of Your Money

Take Control of Your Money

A LIFE GUIDE TO FINANCIAL FREEDOM

Barbara Lee & Paula M. Siegel

VILLARD BOOKS   1986   NEW YORK

Copyright © 1986 by Barbara Lee and Paula M. Siegel
All rights reserved under International and Pan-American Copyright Conventions. Published in the United States by Villard Books, a division of Random House, Inc., New York, and simultaneously in Canada by Random House of Canada Limited, Toronto.

LIBRARY OF CONGRESS CATALOGING-IN-PUBLICATION DATA
Lee, Barbara, 1941–
Take control of your money.
1. Investments.   2. Finance, Personal.   I. Siegel,
Paula M.   II. Title.
HG4521.L334   1986   332.024   86–40097
ISBN 0-394-54392-0

Grateful acknowledgment is made to the following for permission to reprint previously published material:

Dow Jones & Company, Inc.: reprint of tables "Calculating Minimum IRA Withdrawals," and "Estimating Your Benefits." Reprinted by permission of Dow Jones & Company, Inc. © Dow Jones & Company, Inc., 1985. All rights reserved.

McGraw-Hill Publications Company: reprint of table "What You Could Save by Refinancing at 13% for 30 Years." Reprinted from the April 29, 1985 issue of *Business Week* by special permission © 1985 by McGraw-Hill, Inc.

Shearson Lehman Brothers, Inc. and First Marketing Corporation of Florida: retirement chart which appeared in a Shearson Lehman Brothers, Inc. newsletter entitled "Strategy" © Shearson Lehman Brothers, Inc. and First Marketing Corporation of Florida, 1985.

The New York Times: Reprint of tables "Investments Favored by the Tax Laws," and "Types of Mutual Funds," from the May 19, 1985 issue of *The New York Times* © 1985 by the New York Times Company. Reprinted by permission.

Manufactured in the United States of America

9 8 7 6 5 4 3 2
First Edition

Book Design: Beth Tondreau

To Stephanie, my daughter, and to Gladys Rackmil. You both encourage, support, suggest, and applaud.

B.L.

For my father, who taught me that limitations are self-imposed.

P.M.S.

A special thanks to our agent Janet Manus

Contents

Introduction — xiii

Part I
THE BASICS
1. The Financial Generation Gap — 3
2. Your Personal Financial Profile — 10
3. A Financial Primer — 26
4. Tools of the Trade — 35
5. The Spectrum of Investments — 53
6. Financial Stores — 61
7. The Investment Pyramid — 68

Part II
STARTING OUT:
INVESTMENT STRATEGIES FOR AGES 25–45
8. Goals for the Early Years — 79
9. Handling Two Incomes — 94

10. Preparing for Parenthood	110
11. For Single Parents	123
12. Your Insurance Needs	134
13. Retirement Considerations	141

Part III

AN EYE ON THE FUTURE:
INVESTMENT STRATEGIES FOR AGES 45–60

14. Goals for the Middle Years	149
15. Providing for Elderly Parents	163
16. Reviewing Your Insurance Needs	170
17. Reviewing Your Retirement Plans	176
Conclusion	187

Introduction

I walked into a friend's house recently and caught her needlepointing. She held up the pillow she was working on so that I could see the motto: Money is the root of all evil and everyone needs roots.

I hope this book will remove any thoughts of evil about money. Money is an integral part of your life and should be used to make your life better. You already know how to think about food, clothes, housing, and other life necessities. Now it's time to learn how to think about money. Your money should never be idle and you should never be idle in thinking about it. You work hard for your money and it should work equally hard for you.

After a long day at the office, your first priority may not be getting your financial affairs in order. Even more likely you might never have made money management a priority at all. Perhaps you simply put your whole pay check into a checking account. You know you are rewarding Uncle Sam too richly. You probably also realize that you have more money coming out of this account than you are putting in. Now is the time to put these thoughts into remedial action.

Taking control of your money may be compared to starting a personal exercise program—it's never too late to begin either one. There is always time for corrective measures. If you disregarded your budget last month and went into debt on your credit card, you can learn to straighten out these money mistakes and go on from there.

The first important step to financial security is knowing that you want to make that step. This book is a practical one and can be used no matter what your age or financial situation. It is not a book telling you how to make a million dollars in a day or a year. However, it will teach you how to think about your money and how to translate these thoughts into creative and effective action.

The feeling of getting confidence in the world of money is rewarding, not only financially, but emotionally too. It is satisfying to know that you are capable of managing and making decisions for your own money. There is a definite excitement that goes along with the sense of monetary accomplishment.

The information presented in this book is meant to help you begin a lifetime of active participation in both planning for and achieving your present and future financial security. Promise yourself that today you will start taking charge of your own money. Today you will begin to exercise financial responsibility.

—Barbara Lee

Part I

THE BASICS

1
THE FINANCIAL GENERATION GAP

Many of you are intimidated by the world of finance. In fact, you were brought up to think of money as a necessary evil that, if too much attention was paid to it, could lead to a life devoid of the *really* important things. How many times were you told, "Money can't buy you happiness"? Yet, when you reach your adult years, you find that money, in fact, *is* necessary for much of what makes you happy, secure, and healthy. You need money to buy food, rent an apartment, save for a car and a house, invest for your retirement, and secure your children's future.

Money is a critical factor in making your dreams and aspirations come true, yet many of you learn as little about financial management from your parents as you did about sex. Financial matters were always shrouded in mystery. You probably never knew how much your parents earned or how it was allocated to feed, clothe, house, and educate the family. Because money was always a taboo subject, you couldn't learn from your parents' rich experience how to avoid the mistakes they made or repeat their successes.

Even without your parents' direct input, however, you're most likely to pattern your financial management after what you remember your parents saying about money, and the few glimpses you had of their budgeting habits. Those of you whose mothers kept the weekly money in an envelope in the kitchen drawer might find yourselves ten years later stuffing grocery or dry-cleaning money in a kitchen or desk drawer. If your parents kept tidy home files of gas, electric, oil, mortgage, and other monthly bills, you might be likely to develop the same habit of filing paid bills for future reference. And, conversely, if your parents were always rifling through the garbage to find the latest phone bill that was accidentally thrown away, you might grow up to have the same helter-skelter money management habits.

Assuming that your parents were not gamblers or spendthrifts, a certain amount of copying is a good thing. But you have to keep in mind that economic times have changed dramatically in the last twenty years. You are not dealing with the same dollar or with the same purchasing power as your parents. Yet because you were always kept in the dark about finances, you aren't able to think creatively about how to manage your money. Those of you in the financial prime of your lives, however, cannot afford to be untidy or naïve in your money management—a lesson most of you learned in the last decade.

THE COST OF FINANCIAL NAÏVETÉ

Many of you saw your spending power cut in half from the time you started working in the 1960s or 1970s to the present day. Rather than having a better lifestyle after a decade of work, many of you may find yourselves in the same place—or worse off—than you were when you started. And you don't know what you're doing wrong. You work hard. You don't feel like you're spending money on extravagances. But it still seems as if the everyday expenses of clothing, food, and transportation are leaving you without a penny to save for the future.

Part of this economic problem is certainly the high price of inflation that you all have paid in the last decade. But part of the problem is also a lack of money management techniques. While inflation is an enemy common to both your parents' and your generations, today's methods of coping with it are not comparable with those used thirty years ago. Yet, most of you are unfamiliar with financial strategies that will both help you keep more of the money you earn and make the money you keep increase in value. Instead you follow your parents' example and keep your money in the two traditional, now stalemate, accounts: a savings account and a checking account. As a result, many of you have seen your spending money and your savings—what little there was of it—devoured by inflation.

The first step toward a more secure financial future is to understand what has happened to your money in the last decade and why your parents' money management rules are ineffective for today's financial needs.

POSTWAR PROSPERITY

In the 1950s and 1960s, with the exception of a short recession or two, the economic scene in this country was one of growth and prosperity for many people. Interest rates remained stable for many years making long-term planning for savings and spending financially sound. Thirty years ago, you could get long-term mortgages at 4.5 percent. At the same time, you would be earning 3 percent on your savings in the bank, which would keep up adequately with a relatively low inflation rate. Money in the bank, as most parents are fond of saying, was money in the bank.

Today you have to bargain for a traditional thirty-year mortgage. Many banks are more partial to the variable-rate mortgage, which provides them with security in the face of erratic interest rates—rates that defy long-term planning. They are not as keen, however, on offering variable interest rates on passbook savings accounts. Regardless of what is the going interest rate paid for money, you'll be making the same 5 to 5.5 percent on your money in a standard account. Of course you have to take out any bank fees levied. And don't forget income tax. By the time you've paid all the fees, you might end up with less money than you started with.

When you consider what is happening to your savings in a regular savings account, you must also be aware of inflation rates. Your parents had to contend with inflation, too, but the purchasing power of the dollar was greater then, and inflation rates were not nearly as erratic as they have been recently. Today inflation rates can go from single digit to double digits with alarming ease; you have to be nimble in financial maneuvering to come out ahead. For example, if the interest on a savings account is frozen at 5.25 percent while inflation is running at 10 to 12 percent, you are going to be losing more money than you are accruing just by leaving your money in a regular savings account.

Perhaps you decide to protect your assets by investing in a home because real estate is always touted as a good hedge against inflation. When your parents started saving for a down payment, they could predict how much they needed in, say, five years to buy a house and then work toward that goal. That hasn't been true in the last ten years. Skyrocketing real estate costs have made saving for a down payment an exercise in frustration. If you plan to save $7,500 in five years to buy a house, you'll find that you'll need $10,000 for the down payment on the same house by the time you've reached your original goal. Not only the down payment gets bigger, but so do the mortgage payments and taxes. In the end, you're no more in a position to buy the house than you were five years before. And what's worse, the money in your savings account is worth less in real spending value than when you started as well!

AGGRESSIVE ECONOMICS

Basically, the difference between your parents' income-earning years and yours is that your parents could make fixed, long-term financial plans because the base of their economy was more stable. Your financial plans have to be flexible so that they can compensate for the significant shifts in interest and inflation rates common today. You can't leave your money in the benevolent hands of the neighborhood bank. This generation's wage earners have to become active participants in planning for their financial security. They have to be educated consumers in today's diversified investment marketplace.

Most of you, however, rarely concern yourselves with economic trends or recognize financial opportunities. Some of this apathy stems from the notion that financial news and investment opportunities are only for corporate magnates and the wealthy. That one misconception is costing the small investor a great deal of money. Actually today, more than at any other time, the small investor can take advantage of an ever increasing variety of high-earning investment opportunities for an initial investment of $1,000 or, in some cases, less.

Disinterest in financial matters also stems from the long-standing notion that talking about money is vulgar and that money matters are extremely private. Genteel people don't talk about money. They're not really concerned with it. Someone else handles it for them. Therefore, what's happening in the financial world is only of interest to the people directly connected with banking and business. It's this conspiracy of silence about money that fosters financial ignorance and prevents the average wage earner from maximizing his or her income.

Despite this social taboo, however, friends and relatives with some financial sophistication are starting to draw quite a crowd at parties. As down payments on houses and college tuitions soar out of sight, people want to know what they can do with their money to make the new car, the house in the country, or the college educations affordable.

You probably have questions and needs of your own. You know what kind of lifestyle you'd like to have, but despite your enviable salary, you still live from one check to another. What you don't know is how to build yourself an economic base that provides for more than a hand-to-mouth existence. That's what you'll learn to do in this book.

There's no magic in money management. Success comes from thoughtful planning that all of you can do. The real hurdle to get past is a passive attitude toward money. Most people live on what they earn. When the sum goes up, they allocate more money to spend. When the sum goes down, they learn to live on less money. In other words, their money manages them.

In this book, you'll learn how to be in control of your income, how to plan with it to create a secure financial future. You'll learn how to keep track of the money you spend so that you can control the allocation of your income to the goals you've set up. You'll learn about the variety of investment opportunities available to individual investors and how to choose among them for specific needs, such as retirement funds, college tuitions, or support for aging parents. You'll also learn about financial advisors and find out what role they should play in your financial planning.

It is the aim of this book to demystify finances and to give you the sense of financial creativity that each investor needs. Toward this end, you'll find the book arranged in three parts, each of which lays the foundation for the next.

Part I, "The Basics," will provide you with working knowledge of key economic indicators, financial investments, and financial advice. In this section you'll actually start to take control of your money by filling in a Personal Financial Profile that will be your point of reference for your money management strategy.

Part II, "Starting Out: Investment Strategies for Ages 25–45," is a financial guide for meeting goals during the early adult years as well as setting up the groundwork for future needs.

Part III, "An Eye to the Future: Investment Strategies for Ages 45–60," offers advice to help middle-aged readers enjoy their most prosperous years while making sure that their retirement and financial obligations to other family members are all being met.

As you can see from the outline, this book is meant to be a working reference that will help you manage your money throughout your life. You'll find no promises for getting rich quick or for getting something for nothing. However, you will find information and advice that can give you the financial freedom to enjoy your life at every stage without worrying about your security in the future.

You might be puzzled at not finding suggestions for two or three investments that will be guaranteed to give you financial security. Such suggestions are unrealistic on a number of levels, but the primary reasons they usually are unsuccessful are these:

1. There's no such thing as a universal financial portfolio that fits everyone's needs. Your objectives and financial resources are unique, and the answers to your financial problems need to be unique as well. What you need, and what you'll find in the following chapters, is information that will help you shape your financial goals and then find ways of attaining them.

2. Financial needs are in constant flux, and therefore the plans made to meet them must be flexible as well. You can't sit down at thirty years of age and map out a plan of investment for the rest of your life. Opportunities change. The value of investments changes. Tax laws change. And of course, your needs and goals change. The successful money manager is not the one who has the most rigid plan of action, but the one who is astute and flexible enough to update an outmoded financial strategy in order to take advantage of opportunities for the greatest financial gains. Rather than give you a set plan of action, then, this book is meant to help you become a more knowledgeable, involved, and successful money manager.

Money management is a challenge, certainly, but not one to be intimidated by. In fact, once you have the tools and the knowledge you need, planning and revising a strategy for your financial security can be an exciting and satisfying experience. Be bold. You worked hard for your money. Now make it work hard for you.

2
YOUR PERSONAL FINANCIAL PROFILE

Successful money management depends to a great extent on understanding what your financial position is: How much of your salary is locked into scheduled monthly bills? How much is customarily used for entertainment and other discretionary spending? How much can be tied up into longer-term investments? How much into short-term, high-interest investments? How much might be needed for tax-advantaged investments to reduce your tax bill?

To answer these questions and create an economic point of departure for your financial planning, you need to compile a Personal Financial Profile that shows you how and where you spend your money as well as what you owe (your liabilities) and what you own (your assets). In the following chapters, you'll find outlines of recommended financial positions for various life stages. By referring to your profile, you can determine whether or not you are meeting the milestones of financial security for your age group and for your personal goals. If you haven't reached them, you can scrutinize your profile for weak points in your money management that are keeping you from attaining these goals.

The Personal Financial Profile is not a record that you create once and file away for future reference. Your financial condition is anything but static. In most instances, it's a little more volatile than you'd like. Any number of life's major decisions from marriage to retirement can change your income as well as your financial burdens. The value of investments also change over time. In order to be an accurate and useful money management tool, your profile needs to be a living document that reflects the changes in your economic condition from year to year. To keep your profile current, it should be updated annually as well as after major life changes, such as marriage, divorce, the birth of a child, retirement, or death of a spouse.

The profile is most easily constructed from receipts, canceled checks, and bill stubs. If you live mostly on a cash basis and have no defined budget, your profile may be less reliable than one created from records, but it should give you some framework nonetheless.

To create your profile, you'll need your checking account statements, receipts, and bill stubs for at least three months. They needn't be three consecutive months. As a matter of fact, choosing months at different times of the year may give you some insight into changes in your spending patterns that occur seasonally, such as a rise in your gas and car maintenance payments in the summer and a larger food and entertainment bill in the winter.

You'll also need statements concerning any outstanding loans or bills, and records of any investments or valuables you own, such as electronic home equipment, real estate, stocks, bonds, and collectables.

Once you have these records at your disposal, you should be able to find all the figures necessary to fill in the following profile chart. The profile is divided into three sections: living expenses; assets (what you own); and liabilities (what you owe).

PERSONAL FINANCIAL PROFILE

LIVING EXPENSES	MONTH	MONTH	MONTH	TAX DEDUCTIONS
Car Maintenance				
Travel				
Gasoline				
Sales Tax				
Car Insurance Payments				
House Insurance Payments				
Credit Card Payments				
Misc. Loan Payments				
Rent and/or Mortgage				
Gas/Electric				
Phone				
Food/Liquor				
Entertainment				
Doctor Bills				
Pharmacy Bills (R_x & Grooming Prod.)				
Subscriptions				
Dry Cleaning				
Other				
TOTAL				
MONTHLY INCOME				

ASSETS	AMOUNT	LIABILITIES	AMOUNT	TAX DEDUCTIONS
Real Estate		Home Insurance Premium (Annual)		
Stocks		Mortgage		
Mutual Funds		Credit Card Debts		
CDs		Credit Line Debts		
Bonds		Home Equity Loans		
Money Market Accts.		Car Loan		
Checking Accts.		Car Insurance Premium (Annual)		
Savings Accts.		School Loans		
Retirement Accts. (IRA, KEOGH, etc.)		Home Improvement Loans		
Credit Union Accts.		Other Loans		
Trust Funds		Tax Shelter Payments		
Savings Bonds		Margin Accounts		
Art Work		Other		
Precious Metals				
Jewelry				
Home Entertainment				
Computers				
Cars/Boats				
Collection				
Jewelry				
Other				
TOTAL		TOTAL		

LIVING EXPENSES

In this part of your financial profile, you'll itemize your day-to-day living expenses such as rent, entertainment, travel, dry cleaning, laundry, gas, liquor, food, garage, phone, utility, credit card payments, birthday presents, and so on. The living expenses section will help you see what your pattern of spending is. Keep in mind that there is no right or wrong pattern of spending. Everyone has different spending priorities. You might feel that theater tickets and subscriptions to the ballet and opera are important while a friend or relative shrugs them off as frivolous and prefers to put that money toward upgrading a home entertainment system. Both of you are "right" as long as you're comfortable with your spending habits.

Three conclusions can be drawn from the information provided under "Living Expenses." First, you'll compare your expenses with your income to see what is happening to the money you bring home. Second, you'll look at the pattern in your spending to see when you need more money and when you need less. And lastly, you'll tally up your tax deductible expenses during the three months charted on the profile.

To compare your expenses with your monthly income, total them and subtract them (if you can) from your monthly income after taxes. Many of you may be surprised by the gap between what you thought you were spending and what you actually spend in a month. Some of you might find that you earn several hundred dollars more a month than you spend on average, but you can't account for where that money has gone. It's just missing. That's a sign of sloppy money management. To "find" that missing money, budget yourself according to the expenses outlined in your profile and make a point of putting the extra cash in each paycheck into a separate account where it won't slip through your fingers unnoticed.

Others may find that they somehow spend more than they earn, which is probably reflected in growing credit card balances. This is the kind of problem that "double-dippers" (people who use their credit cards when they're short on cash) run into. The intention is to pay back the charged items with the next paycheck. All too often, though, the next check doesn't last long enough either, and the double-dipper resorts to using the credit cards again. People who find this kind of pattern in their spending need to scale down their spending to fit better into their income bracket. A month or two on a strict cash-only basis might give the double-dipper a better sense of what he or she can and can't afford.

Still others may find that they have money left over every month and that their checking account balance has been growing steadily over the last year. However, even these frugal people are losing money by ignoring the fundamental rule of personal finances: Never let your money be idle. A fat checking account balance that earns no interest actually is being eaten away by inflation when it could be growing in a money market fund or some other high-interest account.

Of course, you might not fall into any of these categories. Your comparison of expenses to earnings might highlight some problem unique to your financial situation. Or you might be right on your budgetary target. The point of this exercise is not to fit into a category, but to gain a better understanding of where your income is going so that you can reshape your spending habits if you don't like what you see.

After comparing your expenses to your income, go back over your living-expenses profile again and see if you can find a pattern in your spending. For instance, many people see an increase in spending in April and November due to tax payments and holiday gift buying, respectively. However, each of us probably has other months when our expenses are high on account of a rash of family birthdays and anniversaries, or coinciding due dates for several insurance premiums and tax shelter payments, or health club and other annual membership payments. The object of this exercise is to put your financial needs into better focus so that you can prepare for the "expensive" months in advance by setting aside money in the months when you don't have any unusual costs. Your expenses might rise and fall from month to month, but your salary probably stays the same. You have to make the adjustments in your allocation of the money to meet your changing financial needs.

The last step in scrutinizing your spending habits is to tally up your tax-deductible expenses in the "Tax Deductions" column on the right side of the page. Many of you may be unaware of how much of your money actually goes to expenses that the government allows you to deduct from your income. The following are common tax deductions you should look for in your record of expenses:

- Finance charges on your revolving credit card accounts
- Sales tax on purchases
- Interest paid on personal, home improvement, or auto loans
- Gasoline and car maintenance expenses connected with business travel
- Business telephone calls as well as the sales tax on those calls
- Cost of professional journals, newsletters, or other business-related reading matter
- Professional organization dues
- Contributions to charities or other tax-deductible causes
- Business-related entertainment expenses

Go back through your statements and break out the tax-deductible items from your overall expenses. You may be surprised at how they add up in just the three months recorded in your profile.

Whether you plan to itemize or not, you should keep a current record of your tax-deductible expenses throughout the year so that you give yourself the option to itemize your deductions if they amount to a meaningful sum at the end of the year. Don't cheat yourself by filing a short form when you could save a few hundred tax dollars by itemizing your expenses.

ASSETS AND LIABILITIES

The next two portions of your profile help you establish your overall financial value. Under the heading "Assets," list all of your financial holdings, including real estate, stock, retirement accounts, credit union accounts, savings accounts, checking accounts, money market funds, certificates of deposit, savings bonds, trust funds, valuable paintings or sculpture, silver or jewelry, home entertainment systems, computers, cars, and any valuable collection, such as rare stamps, coins, or books. Next to each item, enter its worth and then add the figures in the column. The total represents what you're worth today.

Under the heading liabilities, list your debts, such as the balance of any outstanding school, car, or home improvement loans, mortgages, total credit card debts, annual household and car insurance premiums, margin accounts (money loaned by a brokerage house against the value of an investment account), and tax shelter payments. Totaling these figures will give you a current picture of your liabilities.

Next to the "Liabilities" column, you'll see a second "Tax Deductions" column. Make sure that any liabilities that are tax deductible are indicated in this column (e.g., tax shelter payments, margin account interest, and mortgage interest).

Rather than reflecting your day-to-day spending habits, the "Assets" and "Liabilities" sections of the financial profile show you the long-range results of your money management or your lack of financial planning. What most people want to see here is that their assets outweigh their liabilities. What many people will see if they are naïve money managers is that their liabilities equal or outweigh their assets. Instead of getting richer, they're getting poorer.

But take heart, those of you who appear to be on the brink of economic ruin. There is no such thing as financial destiny. You have the power to change your course and secure your financial future. You've already taken the first step in a new direction by figuring out your unfortunate current status. However, compiling a financial profile alone is neither going to reduce your taxes and your debt nor increase your worth and your cash flow. The profile simply shows you what money is coming in and where it is going, what you're worth, and what you owe. By setting your finances out on paper, you'll find it much easier to plot a future financial direction—the next step toward reaching your financial goals.

THE FIVE STEPS TO MANAGING YOUR MONEY

The only way to realize a steady growth in your overall worth and to insure that your future financial needs will be met is by developing a money management plan that week to week, year to year leads you to your goals. However, many of you don't know how to map out a financial and investment plan for the future. You're having trouble budgeting your money from one paycheck to the next without the complications of planning for your future security. However, taking control of your finances is not as difficult as it seems. The trick is to master one area of financial concern at a time and build a comprehensive understanding of your economic goals so that a strategy for reaching them can be planned. But what are the important financial concerns that you should learn about? How can you apply what you learn to your money management?

The following Five Steps to managing your money answer those questions. They outline the cornerstones of sound financial planning. These Five Steps are designed to open your eyes to a new way of looking at your money. They will help you look critically at your spending, saving, and investing so that you can reshape your financial habits in such a way that they consistently contribute to the growth of your total worth and help you prepare for future financial obligations.

The Five Steps give you the shell of a management plan that you can then flesh out with your own goals and needs as they evolve during your life. The ability of these Five Steps to be flexible enough to address a variety of changing financial needs is the strength of this management plan. It allows you to keep your financial framework intact throughout your life, using a basic strategy to meet the fluctuating financial obligations of early, middle, and late adulthood.

You'll note in future chapters in this book that advice on financial preparation for specific life situations, such as getting married or having a baby, outside of the basic Five Steps is offered. These additional financial guidelines are meant to be used within the framework provided by the Five Steps, not instead of it. In other words, once you've used the Five Steps to create a financial strategy that will meet your general goals, you can further tailor your plan for significant life changes by using the additional guidelines provided for those situations.

STEP 1: MAXIMIZE YOUR LIQUIDITY.

Everyone needs spending money to draw on for rent, food, utility, and other bills of daily living. In addition, some people need moderate sums of money set aside for regular periodic payments of short-term debts. The income used for these financial obligations needs to be kept liquid, or available for use on demand. Oftentimes, these liquid assets are left in checking accounts that not only pay no interest, but even cost the customer money in the form of maintenance fees. Instead, the funds could be put in a variety of interest bearing accounts, such as money market accounts, NOW accounts, and money management brokerage accounts, that, in exchange for keeping a predetermined minimum balance in the account, accrue interest right up until the day of withdrawal.

For instance, let's say that you get paid twice a month. You pay your bills and your rent on the first of every month. Then you draw spending money as you need it weekly. At the end of the month, whatever is left goes into your savings account. For the better part of the month, you have a large balance that sits in your account without earning a penny of interest.

Instead of this system, you could deposit all of your income into a money market account and draw funds from it as needed. Your savings and your spending money would be earning a high rate of interest up to the day of withdrawal.

There are many combinations of interest-earning money market funds, checking accounts, and certificates of deposit that can be used to put your cash-on-hand to work. Specific investments will be discussed in later chapters.

STEP 2: CONSOLIDATE ASSETS.

The second step of personal money management is more a matter of organization than anything else. Most of us have small amounts of money scattered in various savings accounts, in penny stocks we bought at the advice of one friend or another, in utilities stocks given to us over the years by aunts, uncles, and grandparents, and in savings bonds acquired at those momentous milestones of confirmations, bar mitzvahs, graduations, and marriages.

These small investments may increase in value over time, but their overall worth may not amount to much. For example, if you own ten shares of utility stock that rose in price from $10 a share to $15 a share in the time you held it, you'd increase your money from $100 to $150. That sounds pretty good. However, if you had gathered up all of the cash gifts and balances from forgotten savings accounts so that you could round out your holdings in the utility company to one hundred shares, your profit would have increased from $50 to $500. That growth in value would have been hard to beat by leaving the small balances in passbook accounts earning 5.5 percent interest annually.

Take a few minutes to go through your old papers and see if you've got any hidden assets. Don't forget to ask your parents if they're still holding any savings bonds from your birth or graduations.

STEP 3: KNOW WHERE YOUR MONEY GOES.

As stated before, there is no right way to spend your money. Some people buy houses. Others keep up subscriptions to the opera, the local orchestra, and the theater, and pay today's exorbitant rents. No matter how you decide to spend your money, you should know where your income goes. How much of your monthly budget is spent on rent, food, finance charges, credit card payments, entertainment, travel, and charitable donations? How much seems to disappear?

Familiarity with spending habits is important to the personal money manager for several reasons, the most obvious being that you have to know where your money is going to make sure that it ends up where you want it to. If you think that you're spending about $100 a week on entertainment and find out that the figure in reality approaches $150, you might want to find a way of limiting your entertainment budget more effectively.

Secondly, you need to know how you spend your money in order to make feasible financial plans for the future. For example, assume that you've decided you want to buy a second home. The bank approves your second mortgage based on your ability to pay your scheduled monthly bills plus mortgage payments out of twenty-eight percent of your gross monthly income. But can you afford the house when you consider your unscheduled monthly bills that the bank doesn't take into account, or that some of the mortgage interest may not be fully deductible? Would you have to cut back on dining out, outings with friends, or your new seasonal wardrobe? If you weren't familiar with your daily spending patterns, you might be rudely surprised at how much you'd have to curtail your lifestyle to afford the second home; the label "house poor" is not one to brag about.

Another reason to keep track of your spending habits is to take advantage of any tax deductions due you. You need to keep records and receipts of business-related expenses, contributions, and sales tax, in order to be able to deduct these costs from your income at tax time.

Finally, you need to know where your money goes in order to review and alter your financial goals as time goes on. Your spending priorities at the age of twenty often are measurably different than your spending priorities at thirty-five.

STEP 4: AVOID TAX SHOCK.

The story is a familiar one. You get a raise that not only is reduced by your current tax, but bumps you into a new tax bracket further eroding your salary. Most of us take our yearly tax bath with the resignation of the defeated. Yet a little attention to detail could save us an important amount of money. For instance:

- Are you taking all the deductions allowed you on your tax form, for example, finance charges, sales tax, business expenses?
- Are you taking advantage of any investment plans offered by your employer for which contributions are deducted from pre-tax income?
- Would tax-free investments yield you more after-tax income than taxable investments?

What you want to ask yourself as you look over your personal finances is, "Am I protecting as much of my income from taxes as I can?" This is an entirely legal pursuit. It is your right to pay the minimum amount of tax you legally can. And to that end, the government offers many opportunities to help you keep your income out of the public coffers. Ironically, taxpayers often feel that taking advantage of these tax breaks is cheating, and end up giving the government more than is necessary.

STEP 5: PLAN FOR SHORT-TERM AND LONG-TERM FINANCIAL NEEDS.

Once you've gotten your present day finances under control, you can turn your attention to future needs. What goals do you have for the next three to five years? Do you need a down payment for a condominium or tuition funds for your child? Through various investment tools, you can establish a guaranteed return (e.g., increase in value, interest, dividend) that will provide the funds you'll need in the near future.

For longer-term plans, you have to map out a strategy that will allow you to assign money to targeted funds on a regular basis to your distant goals, such as retirement or a college tuition fund for your children. While these monies are meant for use in the distant future, they can't be left even in the safest investment without further regard. Opportunities for increased earnings need to be assessed periodically in order to assure maximum growth of your funds.

The key word for reaching either short-term or long-term goals is *planning*—making regular contributions to a goal over a specified period of time. Most people groan at the thought of this kind of financial discipline. Actually, it's the most painless method of meeting your financial obligations. Take college tuition, for example. If parents put away $250 a month towards their child's education from the day of birth until age two and invest that money in zero coupon bonds yielding 12 percent a year, they'd have $40,000 by the time the child was eighteen. However, if they waited to address the question until their child was nine years old, they'd have to invest about $13,000 at that time to come up with the $40,000 in nine years.

Now, you've got your Personal Financial Profile and you've read through the Five Steps. But how can you put these two investment tools to work? Take a look at the first step, maximizing your liquidity. On your profile, you listed the accounts where you deposit your liquid assets. What kind of accounts are they? Are they costing you money instead of paying you money for keeping your money in the account? If the answer to that question is yes, you should look for alternative depositories for your liquid money (this is discussed in later chapters).

For the second step, consolidating your assets, you can refer to the "Assets" section of your profile. What kind of investments do you see there? Are there several small savings bonds past maturity? A few shares in several companies given to you as graduation and wedding presents? These are the kinds of small assets that might be consolidated into a larger investment with greater earning potential. Later, as you learn more about what investment opportunities are available and which are best for your situation, you'll be able to choose an investment in which to consolidate your smaller holdings.

If you filled out your Personal Financial Profile, then you've already addressed the third step, knowing where your money goes. You can just glance over your living expenses section to see how your money is spent. However, the follow-up to this step—altering your spending habits to improve your financial position—will take planning based on your current cash flow needs, your tax status, and your age. You'll find guidance on financial planning tailored specifically for your lifestyle, whether you're single, married, beginning a family, or thinking about retirement, in the following chapters.

The fourth step, avoiding tax shock, also is partially addressed in your profile. You've at least begun keeping the records necessary to take any tax deductions coming to you. However, as you learn about the various kinds of income you can earn from investments, you'll be able to take another step toward reducing your taxes by investing in financial products whose earnings are partially or wholly tax free.

The fifth step, planning for short-term and long-term financial goals, can start with a close examination of your total worth and your total debt. What do you own now that will contribute to your future financial security? Do you have some investments that need to be rearranged to provide for a specific goal in the future? Are you so mired in paying off a variety of debts that you have no money to invest toward the future? Finding the answers to these questions will take some creative financial thinking on your part.

You can't think creatively, however, when you don't know what tools are available to help you budget, save, and spend your money more wisely. The following mini-guide to investments and how they work will introduce you to the tools of the trade.

3
A FINANCIAL PRIMER

How does an investor know when to buy and when to sell his or her holdings to get the greatest return? The answer to that question is truly that there is no formula financiers can turn to for direction in their investment transactions. This is in part what makes financial planning exciting as well as fun. The investor has to analyze information about the economy, emerging scientific, medical, industrial, business, and political developments, and performance records of potential investments in order to see trends that will influence financial strategy. Of course, every individual's interpretation of news affecting the financial world is different, so financial strategies will vary from one investor or stockbroker to the next. The challenge, of course, is to forecast a trend that leads to a winning investment strategy and an increase in the investor's financial worth.

But how can you begin to see these trends if you have no experience in the financial world? How do you fit the pieces of information together to find the economic patterns? Market mavens and self-styled financiers may pore over specialized financial newsletters, but don't let their zeal for the intricacies of the financial world scare you off. Most of what you need to know can be found in the local newspaper, weekly newsmagazines, television news shows, and such popular financial publications as the *Wall Street Journal*, the financial weekly *Barron's*, *Business Week* magazine, *Forbes*, and *Fortune*. These sources provide an overview of the most important news that affects the economy and, consequently, your investments. However, you may have to read or watch news coverage from a different point of view, interpreting the report not only for its news value, but for its relevance to the financial world.

For instance, when the cover story in a newsmagazine concerns import quotas and what they mean to U.S. industry, that's information that the investor can use to get a sense of how certain sectors of U.S. industry are doing. Does the reporter say that the quotas are helping U.S. industry? Are productivity, sales, and profits of affected industries up? Or has there been a backlash to these quotas?

In the medical and science areas, new product developments frequently are reported by leading manufacturers in the fields. What electronics company has just reported developing a new microchip? What pharmaceutical company has found a long-sought vaccine? What telecommunications firm has designed a revolutionary means of transmitting information? How are these developments going to affect the individual sectors of U.S. industry? Is it likely that there will be significant investment opportunities arising out of the development, such as when personal computers and word processors were introduced in the last decade? Or will the new product affect only one company's future? What are the reporter's feelings on those questions?

When you come to the business news reports, don't change the channel or turn past the page to the entertainment section. Take a look at what significant mergers are taking place, what industries are suffering losses and why, and what new businesses are flourishing. Oftentimes, the business news reporter will not only tell you what is going on in the industrial world, but how the news is likely to affect both existing and potential investors.

Also, glance over the reports on the economy. Is the stock market active or depressed? Where are investors putting their money? In stocks? Bonds? Mutual funds? Or are they staying in cash? Are interest rates climbing, making money less available to businesses and individuals? Or are they falling, making funds easier to obtain?

At first, the economic and financial news may seem a little alien to you. You might not understand how the information can be useful. Don't be discouraged. If you make a habit of keeping abreast of activity in the financial world, you'll begin to see how upward, downward, and stable trends in the economy can guide your financial planning. To give you a headstart in your financial education, here's a guide to the key economic indicators and influences, and how they affect the financial world at large as well as the individual investor's financial planning.

KEY ECONOMIC INDICATORS AND INFLUENCES

Money Supply: Money supply is a measure of the money in circulation, in savings accounts, and in checking accounts. Every week, usually after the close of the stock market on Thursday, the nation's money supply figures are released. These figures are used to help regulate the supply and demand for money in the nation's economy. How fluctuations in the money supply can affect your investments can best be understood if you think of money as a commodity and interest as the price of the commodity. Think of what happens to a product, like Cabbage Patch Dolls, when the demand grows but the supply stays the same. The price of the product goes up. Conversely, when the demand for the product eases, the price probably will be reduced as an incentive to the consumer. When the demand for money is high and the supply is constant, interest rates normally rise. Likewise, again, when supply is constant and demand is low, rates tend to go down. The supply of money is regulated to a great extent by the Federal Reserve System.

The Federal Open Market Committee (FOMC): The FOMC is responsible for balancing the supply and demand of money by means of raising or lowering interest rates charged by the Federal Reserve to its member banks. If high interest rates make money too expensive, the FOMC may loosen credit by lowering the interest rate. The banks then can lower the interest rate that they charge making the cost of loans easier to manage for industry and for consumers like you. If the money supply seems to be growing out of control, the FOMC may decide to raise the interest rate to tighten the availability of money.

Discount Rate: This is the interest rate charged by the Federal Reserve to its member banks. The member banks in turn base the interest rates they charge customers on the discount rate. Thus, if you hear that the discount rate has dropped a half point or a point, you may expect to hear next that some banks are lowering the cost of their loans.

Prime Rate: The prime rate is the interest rate charged by banks to their most valued customers—large businesses and institutions that have complicated financial needs and active accounts. It usually moves up and down in response to fluctuations in the discount rate. The prime is a key financial indicator because so many other interest rates, such as those for home mortgages, margin interest charges in a brokerage account, and money market daily interest rates are pegged to this one.

The Dow Jones Average: The Dow is the major stock market indicator. This average is a statistical device that shows the general levels and movements of stock prices on the New York Stock Exchange. The Dow is actually made up of four different averages—the industrial, the transportation, the utility, and a composite of all three—but the thirty stocks making up the industrial average are the most widely followed, written about, and discussed.

Though the Dow Jones average is the figure most often reported in economic news briefs, it is important to remember that the average does not reflect the movement of every stock. Many stocks buck the trend and go up when the Dow is resting or going down. And just as many go down when the Dow is breaking new records. The Dow is useful as a barometer of market activity and movement. It can help you determine when the climate is favorable for investing in the market. If the Dow is on a slow but steady decline for a few months, you might want to put your money elsewhere until you see a turnabout. On the other hand, if the Dow seems to be recovering from a low ebb, you might want to move some money into the market to ride the recovery. However, the Dow Jones average can't be depended upon to forecast the future of your investment. When you buy stock in a company, make your investment based on the business's performance, future promise, and return to investors—not on a sudden jump in the Dow Jones average.

Volume of Trading: Usually after giving the Dow Jones average, the financial reporter will mention the volume of trading on the New York Stock Exchange. This is the number of shares either bought or sold on that particular day. The volume is an indicator of investor interest in the stock market. If volume is stagnant or drying up, it means that neither the individual investor nor the institutional investor is putting money into the market. Investors may feel that the stock market may not be the best place to put their money at the moment or they may be waiting on the sidelines trying to sense a new direction to take. Conversely, when the volume turns around and starts back up, it's a sign either of confidence in the stock market's performance or panic in a rush to get out.

New Orders: You can get a reading on the general business climate in the report on *Manufacturer's Shipments, Inventories and Orders*, issued around the twenty-third of each month by the Census Bureau. Both the *Wall Street Journal* and *Business Week* will print these reports. Just look at what's happening to new orders coming into factories. If the figure is rising, future sales should grow, too. If the figure is down, it may be a sign that sales are falling off. Be aware, however, that these figures tend to be volatile. You shouldn't leap to any conclusions on the basis of a couple months' data.

Retail Sales: The *Retail Sales Report*, also issued by the Census Bureau, offers insight into business activity. A healthy level of business is indicated whenever retail sales are going up faster than the inflation rate. Thus, when inflation is running at about 4 percent a year, a monthly gain of 6/10 of 1 percent in retail sales (which would be a gain of more than 7 percent annually) indicates a good retail business. The one caution about this indicator that you should keep in mind is that it frequently is revised quite drastically either up or down after publication. The revised figure is the one you want to use when planning your investment strategy.

Consumer Income: The Commerce Department issues the *Personal Income Report* monthly that reports both growth in consumer income and savings rate. The savings rate is the amount that has remained or has been added to checking, savings, or money-market-type accounts. These reports also can be found in the *Wall Street Journal* or *Business Week* magazine. If the growth in consumer income is rising faster than the inflation rate, consumers have money to spend for goods and services, which stimulates the economy. However, if the savings rate is going down, you should stay alert to the possibility that consumers may be forced to slow down spending in the months to come, which could hurt the economy.

Keeping track of these key economic indicators can be made easier by calling the Office of Management and Budget at (202) 395-3093 for their calendar indicating the dates on which the various government agencies release their economic data.

How do you analyze the movement of these indicators and financial news to help you make decisions about investments? Consider these examples:

- Five years ago, you bought a condominium. At that time, fixed-rate, thirty-year mortgages were at about 17 percent. You opted for a variable mortgage at the lower rate of 15.75 percent. The mortgage had no ceiling on the interest that could be charged over the life of the loan, so it was possible—even if not probable—that the interest could climb above the 15.75 percent in the future. Over the next five years, however, the interest rate on your variable mortage dropped to 12.50 percent, so the variable interest rate worked in your favor. However, at lunch with a friend, you enter a discussion about her application for a variable rate mortgate at 11 percent with a 5 percent increase ceiling over the life of the loan. Unlike your mortgage, hers gave some insurance against skyrocketing interest rates in the future. You decide that the security of the interest cap is worth the cost of refinancing your apartment.

During the time that you are filling out your mortgage application, you notice on the news that the Federal Reserve has lowered its discount rates .5 percent and is likely to lower it the same amount again in the near future. The financial reporter feels that mortgage rates could decline to reflect this lowered rate in the next month or two. That's the kind of news that would directly affect your current financial strategy. Should you go for the 11 percent interest rate now or should you gamble a little and wait to see if the interest rates really do decline? You might give your banker as well as your stockbroker a call and ask what he or she thinks is going to happen in the near future to help you make your decision.

- You just got a $1,500 bonus. It's not money you need for living expenses, so you decide to try your hand at investments. At the time you get this bonus, money market funds are promising interest rates of 16 percent or higher, so you decide to put your cash in a money market fund. However, you notice the following trends in the financial news reports over several months:

    1. Inflation rates running near 10 percent are dropping rapidly. Forecasts suggest that inflation will drop down to 5 percent in the next year.

    2. As the inflation rate eases, the FOMC loosens up credit to spur the economy by providing lower interest rates on loans.

3. As the discount rate and the prime rate fall, you notice that the return on your money market funds is also falling because the fund's interest rates are also tied to the prime.

4. News of the ease in inflation and the lower interest on credit stimulates activity on the stock market. The Dow Jones begins to climb where it had been declining or remaining in a narrow range, and trade volume is up—two signals that investors are optimistic about the stock market's performance for the future.

5. New orders and retail sales reports that reflected stagnation in business and industry begin to take a turn suggesting that the economy is expanding and will continue to do so for a while.

If you take all of these observations into account, you might come to the conclusion that a change in the economic climate is taking place that may make the stock market a good prospect for some of that money you have in the money market fund whose return is decreasing.

Of course, this sequence of events doesn't always follow this pattern. If there were prescribed paths for economic changes, everyone would be able to follow them and you'd have a guarantee of becoming wealthy. Inflation rates can look like they're headed down and interest rates can come down, but only certain sectors of the economy seem to respond to these incentives while others continue to languish for reasons that couldn't have been predicted. At other times, despite all indicators to the contrary, an economic swing up or down occurs. For instance, at the time of this writing, while the economy as a whole is enjoying expansion and the Dow Jones average is going up, the electronics industry is suffering a slowdown. Investors who put their money in this sector when the market turned around probably never realized the gain they expected.

In a way, you can look at the challenge of developing a successful investment strategy as having three parts: 1. to identify correctly the trends early enough to buy a product at the time it will give you the greatest return; 2. to invest your money in a product that responds to the trend you've predicted; and 3. to adjust your investment strategy if the economy reacts differently than you expected or if your investment choice doesn't perform as you expected. Success in financial planning comes less from picking winners than from being astute enough to take advantage of opportunities and flexible enough to revise a losing strategy.

Some of you may wonder how following these financial indicators can benefit you when you're really in the dark about what investment opportunities are out there to let you take advantage of economic trends. To shed some light on that subject, you'll find a thorough description of the many investment opportunities available to you, where you can find information about them, what kind of return you can expect from them, and how they respond to various economic influences in the following chapter.

4
TOOLS OF THE TRADE

By now you have a good overview of your financial status from your Personal Financial Profile, you've become acquainted with the Five Steps for reshaping your financial strategy, and you're beginning to get some insights into the economic and investment worlds. At this point, you need to know what tools are available to help you use this information and plan your financial future.

- What kinds of investments are available?
- What kinds of income or return do these financial products provide?
- Which investments are the safest? Which the most risky?
- Who can help you investigate and evaluate investments?
- Where do you buy the various financial products?
- How can you keep track of your investments' performances?

AN OVERVIEW OF INVESTMENT OPPORTUNITIES

A generation ago, the investment picture for most individuals was a fairly simple one. You might own some utility stock shares and government E or H bonds, but the largest part of your savings was safe in the bank. Today, the competition between banks and investment firms has given birth to a veritable supermarket of investment opportunities even for the small investor. New financial products seem to come on the market every week while others are phased out. For the individual investor trying to keep up with economic opportunities, this kaleidoscope of financial products can be confusing. An easier way to gain a working knowledge of investment opportunities is to become acquainted with the basic categories of investments into which most financial products can be divided. The following overview of investment opportunities will provide you with the information you need to understand most investment opportunities being offered today.

Bonds: Bonds are loans—most often in $1,000 denominations—that investors make to corporations or government bodies. When you buy a bond, you are essentially loaning a company, state, city, or federal agency your money for a predetermined interest rate. For instance, Company X is raising $100,000 by selling bonds worth $1,000 apiece. If you buy a bond, Company X will—to the best of its ability—pay you 10 percent interest over the life of the loan, which is ten years. At the end of the ten years when the bond has matured, you'll get back your $1,000 as well as 10 percent on your money paid to you at semi-annual intervals over ten years. However, you also have the option to sell your bond before it matures if you need the money for some other investment or if you feel that the company is in such bad financial straits that it might not be able to pay you your interest or your principal. Thus, a market is created for bonds. Their prices tend to rise and fall in an inverse direction to that of interest rates. As interest rates fall, bond prices increase, and vice versa.

To help you understand how bond prices can fluctuate, let's suppose that you bought Company X's bond in 1975 when 10 percent was a good return on your money. However, in 1980, Company Y, as well as most other companies, was offering a 16 percent return for a $1,000 bond because interest rates were hovering around that level. If you wanted to sell your bond in 1980, most investors wouldn't be willing to pay you the full face value (known as par) of $1,000. After all, they could get 16 percent from many other companies for that investment, so why settle for 10 percent? However, investors might be more attracted to your sale if the par value were discounted to, say, $600. Then they would be able to buy your $1,000 bond for $600, accrue the 10 percent interest on the face value of the bond for the remaining five years, and receive the full $1,000 principal payment at the end of that time. The lowered price would make the lower return more palatable. The opportunity for a long-term capital gain from $600 to $1,000 per bond would also be attractive.

On the other hand, what if interest rates dropped to 7 percent in the five years after you bought your $1,000 bond? Then you'd be able to sell your bond at a premium. A buyer might be willing to pay you $1,300 per bond for the privilege of locking in a higher interest rate than is being offered at the present time.

The quality of a bond is directly related to the ability of the borrower to honor the debt. In order for investors to have some guide to the quality of a bond before they buy it, most bonds are rated. Moody's and Standard & Poor's provide the ratings used most often by investors. Moody's highest rating is Aaa. This would go to bonds that are guaranteed, like treasury bills, bonds, and notes from the federal government. The ratings go down from there to Aa, A, Baa, and so on. Standard & Poor's ratings are similar with AAA being given to the highest quality bonds. Lesser bonds would be rated AA, A, BBB, BB, B, and so on.

The safest investment for a bond buyer would be an AAA or Aaa rated bond, but this would not necessarily be the most lucrative investment. Some of the lesser-rated bonds can bring in a better return, though they are a bit riskier. For instance, if interest rates are currently at 10 percent and a corporation with a lower credit rating needs to borrow money, it might float a bond with an 11 percent interest rate in order to entice the investor.

Aside from looking at the rating of a bond, an investor should pay attention to the call feature sometimes allowed to the borrower. If a bond is "callable," the borrower has the right to redeem the bonds earlier than the maturity date given, thereby cutting short the term during which you'll receive interest. A company may use the call feature if interest rates fall substantially over the life of a given bond. If it is more profitable to redeem the old bonds and issue new ones at the lower prevailing rate, a company will redeem the old bonds. The call date, the earliest date at which time the borrower may redeem the bond, is available to the investor at the time of purchase. If you're looking for long-term income, you may want to make sure that the bond you buy has no call feature or a call feature late enough in the life of the bond to make the investment still attractive to you.

If you've bought a bond, you should keep track of its trading value (the amount of money it can be bought or sold for). You can find this information in the bond table listings in the financial pages of some local papers or in the *Wall Street Journal*. These listings are really easy to understand once you know what the different columns of figures stand for. Here's a sample you can use to decipher bond listings:

Bonds	Cur Yld	Vol	High	Low	Close	Net Chg.
IBM9⅜04	10.	247	92	91⅜	92	+¼

The first three letters, IBM, is the abbreviation of the corporation's name—in this case International Business Machines. The first figure, 9⅜, is the interest you'd receive annually on the face value of the bond. That's your annual actual *return*—the interest you receive on this investment. The second figure, 04, is the abbreviation for the date at which the bond matures. In this case, the date is 2004, abbreviated customarily to the last two digits of the year. The third figure, 10., a percentage, refers to the yield-to-maturity of the bond—the total return (interest plus capital gain) on your investment if you were to hold the bond until maturity. The fourth figure tells you the total dollar amount of bonds traded on that day. The figure represents thousands of dollars, so the volume for this day would be $247,000 when you add in the missing three zeros, or in simpler terms, 247 bonds traded.

The next four figures tell you about the price of the bond during the day's trading activity. These figures also are abbreviated and actually represent tens of dollars. Thus, the first figure, 92, represents $920.

The first figure, 92, is the highest price the bond was sold at during the day. The second figure, 91⅜, is the lowest price. The third figure, 92, is the price paid for the bond when the market closed for the day. The final figure reflects the change in value of the bond from yesterday's close of trading to today's closing price. In this case, the bond gained $2.50 in value from the close of yesterday's business to the close of today's business. This last figure is the one that will show you the bond's performance over a period of time if you follow it regularly.

Bonds issued by the U.S. Treasury, such as U.S. Treasury bills, notes, and bonds are listed in separate tables. Notes and bonds give information in a style similar to the bond listing example above. U.S. Treasury bills, however, are listed in a slightly different manner. Here's a sample listing:

U.S. Treas. Bills

Mat. date	Bid	Asked Discount	Yield
1985			
7–11	7.24	7.10	7.20

Treasury bills (T-bills) are sold at a discount from face value. The yield, or income paid on your investment, is the difference between the discount price you pay and the face value of the T-bill that you'd receive at maturity. As the bond matures, the discount decreases, and the difference between the buying price and the face value decreases. Therefore, the overall yield of the T-bill changes. The listing reflects the fluctuations in yield over the life of the T-bill. The first figure is the maturity date of the T-bill. The next figure, the discount bid, gives you the yield you would receive if you were to sell the T-bill on the date of this listing. The third figure is the discount yield at which you would be buying the bill on this date. And the final figure is the total yield on your investment if you were to buy the bill today and hold it to maturity.

Convertible Bonds: These are corporate bonds that give the buyer the option of converting the bond into stock at a later date. The advantage of a convertible bond is that you get the security of a regular return on your investment but can take advantage of a company's prosperity as well. Because a convertible is a bond, you will receive the stated coupon rate of interest as long as you hold the bond. The bond also has a conversion formula for a certain number of shares of common stock of the offering company. Therefore, if the company is faring well, you may decide to forego the bond interest, convert your bond into common stock and participate in the company's prosperity through increased stock prices. In most cases you may convert at will any time before the bond's maturity date.

Stocks: A stock is a share of ownership in a corporation. If Company X is offering one hundred shares of ownership in its corporation and you buy ten shares, you'll own 10 percent of the company. When the demand for stock in a company goes up, such as when a popular new product is developed and promises to boost sales and profits, the price of the stock should go up. When the demand for stock in a company goes down, such as when a key product becomes obsolete and drives down sales and earning, the price of the stock goes down.

Corporations sell basically two kinds of stocks, common and preferred. Common stocks are the shares of ownership described above and make up the bulk of stocks sold to investors. Preferred stocks combine characteristics of a bond and a common stock. They represent ownership like common stock, but they have the advantage of a bond's stated rate of return, meaning that the holder of the preferred stock will receive a predetermined amount of money (dividends) annually for each share owned. Common stock can also pay dividends, but the amount paid may fluctuate.

Some preferred stocks act like convertible bonds in that they can be converted into common stock if the company prospers and the price of the common stock rises. If the company is prosperous, the price of the preferred stock obviously will also rise in value, but not as rapidly as the common stock because of the high dividend return. For those looking for current income, however, holding onto preferred stock is recommended rather than converting to the lower-yielding common stock because of the high dividend.

In the event of a bankruptcy, preferred stock owners would be second in line to receive their invested money—after bond holders and before common stock owners. Of course, for these added attractions, preferred stocks also carry a higher price tag than common stock.

If you owned stocks, you'd want to track their fluctuations in value in the stock listings either in your local newspaper or in the *Wall Street Journal*. To do this, you'd need to know where the stock is traded—on the New York Stock exchange, the American Stock Exchange, the OTC (over-the-counter) market, or on a regional exchange. When you purchase stock, that's one question you should be sure to ask. Once you find the correct listing, look for the name of your company. Finding the name can be tricky because the stock's name is abbreviated in the listing, but the names are alphabetized according to actual spellings. Thus, in the listings below, "CstlC pf" looks like it should come after "CatrpT", but actually comes before it because "CstlC" stands for Castle & Cooke, and "CatrpT" stands for Caterpillar Tractor.

52-Week		Stock	Div.	Yld.	P-E	Sales	high	low	close	Net
high	low			%	Ratio	100s				change
33	15¾	CstlC pf		13.2	--	42	19	18⅜	19	+⅞
52¾	28⅜	CatrpT	.50	1.5	--	1247	32⅞	32⅝	32⅞	+⅛

The listing is for the corporation's common shares, unless a special abbreviation follows the name. The abbreviations are explained in a box that appears somewhere in the stock pages. A common abbreviation is "pf," which appears after "CstlC" in the example and means the listing is for preferred stock.

The two left-hand columns of the listing show the stock's fifty-two week high and low. This tells you what the trading range has been for the past year—Caterpillar's was between $28⅜ and $52¾ a share—and you can see immediately whether the stock is near its high, its low, or somewhere in between. On this particular day, Caterpillar was trading around $32, close to its low for the year.

The first column after the company's name indicates the annual dividend per share paid out by the corporation to its stockholders. Caterpillar's current dividend is $.50. In the next column is the yield, the percentage of the stock price accounted for by the dividend. Caterpillar's yield is 1.5 percent (32⅞ × .015 = $.50).

Yield gives you a basis on which to compare the income you'll receive from this investment relative to others you might be considering. If you're looking for current income, you'll want the greatest yield possible.

A stock's income-producing ability isn't the only criterion by which to measure an investment's attractiveness. In fact, current income may be less important to you than its potential for price appreciation, depending on the goal of your investment.

In the next column normally would be a figure for the "P-E Ratio," which describes the relationship between a stock's price and its earnings. The figure is obtained by dividing the current price by the company's earnings per share for the past twelve months. A stock selling for $50 a share and earning $5 a share has a P-E

Ratio of 10 to 1. This figure gives you a common denominator with which to measure a stock's value when compared with others in the same industry. You'll note in the Caterpillar listing above that this company has no P-E Ratio listed, indicating that the company had no earnings over the past year. The investor will have to gather further information on the reason for the lack of reported earnings either from the corporation itself, or from a financial consultant. Perhaps the company had been near bankruptcy and is turning around now.

The next column reflects the volume of shares traded on that business day. The figure represents hundreds of shares traded, so the figure 1247 actually represents 124,700 shares.

The last four columns are similar to the last four columns in bond listing. 32⅞ refers to the highest price of the day, 32⅝ to the lowest price, and 32⅞ to the closing price of the stock. The figure in the last column, + ⅛ reflects the change in price from yesterday's closing to today's closing. Today, Caterpillar rose ⅛ or 12.5 cents. As in the case of bond listing, this final figure is the one to watch to follow the performance of your stock.

Options: An option is the right to buy (or sell) a certain stock at a certain price during a predetermined period of time. Essentially, an option is a wager. Instead of buying the stock outright, you're buying a bet that the stock will rise (a call), or that it will fall (a put). If you bet correctly your option appreciates in value and you come out ahead. If you bet incorrectly, you stand to lose part or all of your investment.

Each option purchased is worth one hundred shares in a company. Options are bought at a strike price—the price at which a stock may be acquired or sold from the option seller—and have a life of three, six, or nine months. When the option expires, it is worthless. For example, stock in Company A is currently selling at $15 a share. You get a tip that the stock is likely to rise to $20 in the next two months. You're not really interested in buying shares in the company, but you wouldn't mind buying a call option at a

$15 strike price. If the price indeed does rise to $20 in two months, your option to buy the stock at $15 will increase in value. If, however, the price of the stock goes down, the value of your wager will also go down, though you will never lose more than your initial investment.

Put options work in the opposite manner. You're buying an option to *sell* stock at a strike price that you expect will be above the market price of the stock. The farther the price falls, the more your option will be worth. However, if the stock rises in value, your option becomes worth less.

Almost all options are listed and can be found in the financial pages of your local paper or the *Wall Street Journal*. Here's a sample listing from the American Exchange:

Option & NY Close	Strike price	Calls-Last Aug	Nov	Feb	Puts-Last Aug	Nov	Feb
A S A 48½	45	4⅝	5¾	6⅝	¾	1⅝	2¼

ASA is the name of the company. Following the name is the closing price at the end of the New York trading day, $48.50 per share. The strike price is $45. Aug, Nov, and Feb represent the months when the respective calls and puts expire. Beneath these dates are the values of the options expiring in those months. For instance, calls expiring in November can be purchased for 5.75 per share. However, as mentioned above, the usual unit of sale is one hundred shares, so you'd multiply the listed price by 100 to get the current price of the option. You would buy one of these calls if you felt that the price of ASA would be higher than 45 in November. Puts for February cost $225 per hundred shares. You'd purchase that investment if you felt that the price of ASA was going to fall below the strike price by February.

Mutual Funds/Unit Trusts: Mutual funds, also known as unit trusts, pool money of individual investors to take advantage of the financial opportunities available to large investors. One of the most common examples of a mutual fund is the money market fund that became so popular in the late 1970s. These funds offer substantially greater interest than regular savings accounts by pooling individual deposits to buy short-term, high-yielding securities ordinarily unavailable to the individual investors because of the large initial investment. Because the money market funds specialize in very short-term investments, you don't have to tie up your money in the fund for any specified period of time to get the higher return. Interest is paid from day of deposit to day of withdrawal. Thus, the money market fund is an optimum place to hold your liquid assets—money you need to have on hand—because it gives you a high rate of return and access to your money at the same time.

Mutual funds are created by companies that sell shares of stock and then use the money from the sales to invest in other securities. A company may offer one mutual fund or a family of funds each with different financial purposes. The kind of investments made by the company will be determined by the purpose of the mutual fund or funds. In the case of money market funds, the purpose is to avail small depositors of high interest rates on their liquid assets. Other mutual funds offer investors tax-free returns by trading in securities whose interest is tax exempt. If you were to break down the three overall goals of mutual funds they would be:

Income: Funds whose investments are aimed at providing a steady income for the investor either of a taxable or tax-free nature.

Growth: Funds whose aims are increasing the financial worth (or dollar value) of the initial investment without necessarily providing any current income (regular return, i.e., interest or dividends).

Combination Growth/Income: Funds whose returns are less than income funds but perhaps equal to a savings bank's return that also offer the potential for an increase in dollar value of the original investment.

The variety of mutual funds is virtually endless, however, because funds frequently have more than one goal in order to offer the investor a combination of benefits within a wide spectrum of risk. In the following chart, the most common categories of mutual funds are outlined.

Type of Fund	Objective
Growth	Seek primarily capital growth by investing in stocks with better than average earnings growth
Fixed-Income	Seek current income; normally invest at least 75% of their assets in bonds or preferred stocks
Growth and Income	Combine capital growth with a requirement for level or rising dividend income
Capital Appreciation	Seek maximum capital growth; often use investment techniques with greater than ordinary risk
Equity Income	Seek safety and high current income by investing in high-yield stocks
Global	Invest at least 25% of their portfolio in foreign securities; may own U.S. securities as well
Small-Company Growth	Aim for capital growth by limiting their investments to companies of a specific size
Option-Income	Try to increase current income by writing covered options on at least half of their portfolio
Balanced	Seek to preserve capital with a portfolio typically 60% in stocks, 40% in bonds
Gold	Invest half of their assets in such gold-oriented stocks as mining companies or finance houses
Specialty	Limit their investments to a specific industry; also called sector funds
Income	Seek high current income by committing a large part of their portfolio to fixed-income securities either taxable or tax-free
International	Invest in securities whose primary trading markets are outside the U.S.
Natural Resources	Invest more than half of their assets in natural resources companies
Option-Growth	Seek to increase asset value by investing at least 5% of their portfolio in options
Socially Conscious	Investment philosophy based on social, political, or environmental ideals

Source: James C. Condon. "Mutual Funds Offer Cacophony of Innovation," *New York Times*, 19 May 1985.

Shares of mutual funds can be purchased through a fund itself or through a broker. Usually, shares purchased from the fund directly are no-load funds, or funds that don't charge a commission although you may be charged a small management fee. Shares of mutual funds purchased through a broker usually require a sales charge or commission. These funds are called load funds.

Whether or not a mutural fund is a load or no-load fund is part of the information you can obtain from the listing in the financial pages. A mutual fund listing might look like this:

	NAV	Offer Price	NAV Chg.
Shearson Income Fund	80.66	N.L.	+.13

The first number after the name of the fund is the net asset value (NAV) of the fund. This is the price at which you can buy a share in your mutual fund. In the next column, the letters N.L. mean that this is a no-load fund. (If it were a load fund, a different, slightly higher price would be given as the cost of purchasing shares in the fund. The difference in prices for buying and selling are accounted for by the sales commission charged by the brokerage firm.) In the last column is the NAV change, which tells you the change in the price of the shares. In this case, the shares gained $.13 in value.

Money market mutual funds are listed separately from other varieties, and the listing for these funds is also different. It would look like this:

Fund	Avg mat.	7/day Yld.	30 Day Yld.	Assets
Shrsn Daily Div.	40	7.35	7.37	3537.9

In the first column is the name of the fund. The second column tells you the average length to maturity of the fund's holdings in days. In the third column is the average seven-day yield or interest. The fourth column indicates the average thirty-day yield, and the fifth column tells you the total assets in millions of dollars.

Certificates of Deposit: Certificates of Deposit (CDs) are documents stating that you agree to leave a predetermined amount of money in an account for a specified amount of time in return for a predetermined amount of interest. Usually, the longer you leave the money in the account, the greater the return on your investment. If you withdraw your money before the maturity date, however, you'll be penalized.

The interest rates or yields of CDs don't appear in the financial pages. CDs usually are purchased through banks or brokerage firms. Their current yields often are advertised in bank windows or in "tombstone" advertisements in the financial pages.

Tangible Assets: These investments aren't traded like stock or bonds, nor do they promise a regular return like CDs. However, tangible assets can gain considerably in value over the life of their ownership. Their value, also, is usually internationally recognized and independent of any specific economy. Thus, tangibles can be a safe investment during economic turmoil when stocks, bonds, and currency itself may lose a significant amount of their value. Tangible assets include jewelry, antiques, china, silver, and any other valuable that can be collected. The only way to keep track of the worth of these investments is to have them appraised periodically and to keep track of the price at which other people with similar assets are selling their tangibles.

Real Estate: Most of you are familiar with real estate as an investment. You buy a home, for instance, and it appreciates in value over the years that you own it. The increase in value may keep pace with inflation or may not. The hope is that when you sell your property, it gives you a good return on your initial investment because you sell it for a price significantly greater than you bought it for. When real estate values are climbing, investing in buildings other than a primary residence is an attractive option for some people. Real estate investments vary greatly. For instance, you can own a two-family house and rent out the apartments. You can be a part of an investment group that renovates apartment buildings and then sells the apartments as condominiums or cooperatives.

Or you can own undeveloped land that you feel has future potential as a development site. Real estate investment also figure largely in tax shelter programs (see the section on tax shelters).

Tax Advantaged Investments: This category includes investments whose returns are either tax-exempt or tax-deferred. One of the most common examples of a tax-advantaged investment is the Individual Retirement Account (IRA), now available to every employee and every employee's spouse. When you make a contribution to your IRA, the amount you deposit is a tax deduction for the current tax year. That's one tax advantage. Secondly, the income and increase in value of the assets in your account won't be taxed until you begin to withdraw money, any time after age 59, at which time you might be in a lower tax bracket. In other words, the tax on the income is *deferred* until you begin withdrawals.

An investment whose return is tax-exempt doesn't give you a tax deduction for your investment, but does give you the benefit of tax-free returns. For a person in a 30–50 percent tax bracket, tax exempt returns can increase greatly the income from an investment. For example, let's say you are in the 50 percent bracket. You have the choice of putting $1,000 in a certificate of deposit for one year and earning 10 percent on your money, or putting the $1,000 in a tax-free money market account earning 7.5 percent in a year. At first glance, the CD might look like the more profitable investment. However, think of the tax consequences. You'd actually be able to keep only 50 percent of the $100 you made on your investment, or $50. The rest would go to Uncle Sam. If you put your money in the tax-free money market account, you'd get a return of $75 rather than $100, but, if the fund were triple tax-free (meaning tax-exempt on local, state, and federal levels), you'd be able to keep the whole $75. You'd have a $25 larger return than you would if you'd put the money in the taxable CD.

The following chart lists the most common tax-advantaged investments as well as what kind of tax advantage they give the investor, tax-deferred or tax-exempt income.

Tax Shelters: Tax shelters are investment vehicles whose first pur-

INVESTMENTS FAVORED BY THE TAX LAWS

Investment	U.S. Exempt	State, Local Exempt	Defer* Income	Special Candidates	Comments
Treasury bills	✔	✔			
Treasury notes and bonds	✔				
Savings bonds (EE & HH)	✔	✔		Those who want to force themselves to save through a payroll deduction program; those in a high bracket now and near retirement, after which they will be in a much lower bracket.	EE's pay 85 percent of the average yield on five-year Treasury securities. HH bonds, only available through an EE exchange, pay 7.5 percent.
Obligations of Federal Farm Credit and Home Loan Banks		✔			
Municipal bonds and notes, available through unit trusts, or bond funds (including money-market funds), or as single bonds or short-term notes—RAN's, TAN's etc.	✔	✔		Depends on yield and bracket. A 9.5 percent yield in a 26 percent bracket is equivalent to a taxable yield of 12.8 percent; in a 50 percent bracket it is equivalent to 19 percent. Proposed flat tax would adversely affect it.	Insured bonds are sold, but the yield is reduced about three-tenths of a percentage point.
Individual Retirement Accounts			✔	Employed persons and spouses	Can earn high, taxable income. Tax deferred until payout begins—at which time other tax benefits may be available. Salary-reduction plans would be discontinued under new tax proposals.
Keogh accounts			✔	Self-employed persons	
Salary-reduction plans			✔	Employees of companies with plans	

Deep discount corporate and Federal bonds	✔	Converts ordinary income into long-term capital gains. Be careful if issued after July 1, 1982.
Six-month certificate of deposit	✔	Bank obligations—may be covered by F.D.I.C.

* The deferral of income is subject to certain elections available to taxpayers and to new laws concerning securities with "original issue discount."

Source: Laventhol & Horwath

Source: Adapted from "Deferring Income and Other Tax-Saving Plans," *New York Times,* 19 May 1985.

pose is to provide significant tax deductions for the taxpayer and whose secondary (and equally important) purpose is to provide some capital, or financial, gain in the future. Many people misconstrue tax shelters as rigged investments that the rich use to evade taxes. Instead, these shelters are investments built around the government's own tax incentives for certain industries. And today, these shelters are not only for the rich, but for many individual investors who have accumulated $5,000 in their savings and can put that money toward a long-term capital gain while getting the benefits of a certain number of tax deductions. If a shelter isn't designed to give you a return on your money, then it probably isn't a well-conceived investment or tax shelter.

The following chart is a summation of this overview of investment categories. The chart will help you compare their types of return available to you.

Each of the various types of investments you've been introduced to in this chapter has its place in a financial plan. Safe investments help secure your future, but investments with some risk offer a greater return. Which investments are considered the safest? Which carry the most risk? A description of possible investments in the next chapter will answer those questions.

INVESTMENT CATEGORIES AND KINDS OF RETURN

	CAPITAL APPRECIATION	*INCOME*	*TYPE OF INCOME*
Bonds	(if discount bond)	X	Interest
Treasury Bills		X	Tax savings, interest
Stocks	X	X	Dividends
Options	X		
Mutual Funds	X	X	Dividends/interest
Real Estate	X	X	Tax savings
Tax-Advantaged	X	X	Tax Savings
Tax Shelters	X	X	Tax savings
Convertible Bonds	X	X	Interest
Tangibles	X		

5
THE SPECTRUM OF INVESTMENTS

Within the broad categories listed in the last chapter is a spectrum of financial products that you can use to tailor your portfolio to your specific needs and investment temperament. Investment temperament refers to your preference either for secure investments with modest returns and guaranteed safety of principal, or for more risky ventures that give you a shot at larger profits but don't insure against loss of principal, or for a mixture of both. Your specific needs will change as your life circumstances change, but your investment temperament may stay the same throughout your life, and it will have a great bearing on your financial strategy.

To help you appreciate the level of risk inherent in various investments, the following guide to financial products currently available is organized according to level of risk, ranging from "very conservative," meaning total security of principal and guaranteed return, to "risk," meaning chance for great profits as well as greater losses.

LEVEL 1: VERY CONSERVATIVE

In this category, there is little or no risk to your principal. No risk means that the initial investment remains static as there is little or no growth in principal associated with these investments. What you do accomplish here is a fixed income generated by your fixed principal.

Investments in this category include money market funds, certificates of deposit, Treasury bills, and savings bonds. Both Treasury bills and savings bonds are bought at a discount and mature at par (full face value). All of these securities offer a guaranteed interest that can be paid either monthly, semi-annually, or at maturity. Initial investments can be as little as $25 for a savings bond to as much as $10,000 for a Treasury bill, so just about every investor can find an affordable entry position.

Certificates of Deposit: A document verifying a deposit of your money made for a specified period of time with specific interest to be paid to you. Minimum investment approximately $2,500.

Treasury Bills: Securities issued by the federal government at a discount (less than face value) that mature in three, six, or nine months. Minimum investment $10,000.

Savings Bonds: A kind of bond issued by the U.S. government. The person who buys a savings bond agrees to lend money to the government for a certain length of time at a set interest rate. Minimum investment $25.

LEVEL 2: CONSERVATIVE

On the conservative level, the highest return is the goal. To attain that goal, the investor is willing to endure a modest amount of fluctuation in the value of the principal, but not enough to suggest any real risk to the initial investment.

In this category, you'll find the highest-rated bonds, either corporate or government. Many federal government agencies offer bonds guaranteed or insured against default. Agencies include the Treasury, the federal home loan bank, the federal farm credit, the government national mortgage association, the federal national mortgage association, and the federal home loan mortgage corporations.

Municipal bonds are issued from local governments and authorities and fall into two broad categories: general obligation bonds and revenue bonds. General obligation bonds are issued by state and local governments, which borrow money this way to build roads, schools, and other facilities. Revenue bonds are issued by power, sewer, industrial development, or other local authorities to secure funds for building and other needs.

AAA-Rated Bonds, Tax-Free Bonds, or Government Bonds: All of these are in essence written promises made by the borrower to repay a specified amount of interest for a specified length of time and to repay the loan on the expiration date or at maturity. Minimum investment is $5000–10,000.

Zero Coupons on Certificates of Deposit, Municipal Bonds, and Treasury Obligations: Zero coupons are deeply discounted notes that mature at face value but accrue no interest. Minimum investment varies with the maturity length, but begin as low as $250–$500. Zero coupons are favored for long-term goals because they provide substantial return with a relatively low initial investment. Zero coupons are available from business concerns as well as from banks and the Treasury, but the Treasury coupons are the most secure and therefore the only type included in the conservative category.

LEVEL 3: MODERATE

The investor in the moderate category is looking for growth and income, whereas the more conservative counterparts are looking only for income. To achieve growth of the principal, however, the investor has to be willing to invest in securities that are not as failsafe as government notes and bonds. However, to offset the increased risk, one looks for a return in the form of dividends or interest that at least equals a savings bank rate of interest—about 5.5 percent. Moderate investments are popular because they offer the investor a total return, that is, income plus growth.

Corporate Zero Coupons: Discounted coupon bonds that mature at par. Minimum investment: variable depending on maturity. Corporate zero coupons offer the same deep discount of government coupons and are issued by corporations that have good investment quality ratings. Blue-chip stocks, such as those in the Dow Jones industrial average, offer good dividends and long histories of increased value of the stock.

Blue-Chip Stocks: Highest-ranking stocks with a long history of earnings despite market fluctuations. Companies have provided uninterrupted payment of quarterly dividends for many years, are leaders in their industry, and have good prospects for growth. There is no minimum investment.

Nonnuclear Utility, Bank, and Insurance Stocks: Nonnuclear utility, bank, and insurance stocks are good income-producing stocks that currently offer a fair amount of security for your investment.

Income-Focused Mutual Funds: Income funds focus on current return with modest growth and invest in more traditional companies. The risks involved with income funds are modest, making this type of fund attractive to the moderate investor.

LEVEL 4: MODERATE RISK

Don't let the term "risk" put you off this category of investments. In today's market, it is not necessarily a pejorative term. The term refers not to a speculative investment, but to any investment that doesn't yet have a proven record of return, such as stocks in a new company. Often, the price of stock shares in a company just going public is low in order to induce investment. The stock may move higher immediately. More often, however, patience is needed for the anticipated gain. The risk you take, obviously, is that the venture might not succeed, and you might lose some of your investment.

There is room in just about every portfolio for moderate-risk or risk investments. The amount of money you put into those categories will depend on how much you can afford to set aside for long-term gains, and, in the event of the worst outcome, how much you can afford to lose.

Choosing an investment in this category is not akin to choosing numbers for a lottery. Information about moderate-risk investments is available so that an evaluation of the security can be made.

Growth Stocks: Stocks in companies with great earnings potential or in companies whose growth has exceeded the rate of the economy's growth or of other corporations' growth. When investing in growth companies, you're going to look for steady increase in sales and earnings over the life of the business.

Discount Bonds: Bonds selling below face value ($1,000). In buying discount bonds, you're going to look for quality bonds that were originally issued when lower interest rates prevailed and now carry a low price. For instance, some telephone bonds that were issued about fifteen years ago with a 3.5–5 percent interest (coupon) rate might be selling today at close to half their face value because of the low return. If you were to buy a $1,000 bond at $500 and hold it until maturity—say five years—you would receive a yield-to-maturity return over 10 percent because you'd be earning 3.5–5 percent a year on the face value ($1,000) of the bond, not on your invested $500. You also double your principal because when the bond returned, you'd receive the par value of the bond rather than the discount price you bought it for.

Tax Shelters: Tax shelters fall into this group because there is the risk that the investment objectives of a shelter will not be totally achieved. For instance, in a real estate program, a foreclosure might occur. In that situation, your money would be returned to you as ordinary income—not capital gain—and the tax benefits of the previous years may be disallowed. When preparing to invest in a shelter, remember to examine the investment merits, the reputation of the general partner and the financing, and the actual tax benefits to you. As was said before, all investments are made in order to make money, not just to save in taxes.

Appraised Tangibles: Real estate, gold, art, jewelry, coins, stamps, and so on. The risk in acquiring real estate or collectibles can be reduced significantly by buying through a recognized dealer or auction house so that you have an expert's appraisal of the value of the property. If bought under these conditions, the investment falls into this moderate-risk category.

Social Investment Mutual Funds: Mutual funds whose holdings reflect a specific set of political ideals, for intance, environmentalism or nuclear disarmament. Social investment mutual funds fall into the moderate-risk level not because the funds focus on growth investments, but because such politically motivated funds have had a short life and, therefore, no track record to recommend or condemn them.

LEVEL 5: RISK

Risk investments are opportunities that allow for a small initial investment made in the hope of a high return. The return, unlike in the previous categories, cannot be predicted by a record of sales and earnings, or by an expert's opinion. Often, it depends on an intuitive feeling that grows out of long-term experience in the area of investment.

Junk Bonds: Bonds that have a low price because the holding company is in financial trouble. Often, when a company is in financial trouble, such as International Harvester (today renamed NAVISTAR) was, the bonds outstanding are sold for a fraction of their price to investors who believe that the company's future is not as bleak as the sellers think it is. The buyer believes that the price of the bonds will climb in the future. Investors in these bonds would have to have background information about the individual company or some knowledge of the business involved on which to base their investment decision.

Unappraised Tangibles: Background knowledge also is a necessity when buying property or collectibles without the help of a professional appraiser. However, hobbyists who have long experience collecting coins, stamps, art, or even investing in real estate may have as much or more insight into investments in their area of expertise than a broker who doesn't share the avocation.

For instance, let's say that you live in New York City and rent an apartment in an established neighborhood. However, for several years as a student, you lived in a run-down building on the Lower East Side. You still go down there to go shopping now and then, so you've kept in touch with the old neighborhood. Lately, you've begun to notice a lot of renovation activity on your old street, and a walk around other streets confirms your suspicions that the area is taking a turn for the better. You see new stylish shops opening, or you notice that formerly unkempt buildings now sport window boxes and newly painted façades. On the basis of your experience in the neighborhood and your understanding of real estate development in New York City, you begin looking for a cooperative or condominium to buy before the area becomes hot property. The risk, however calculated, is significant because of the unpredictable nature of real estate values. However, because of your knowledge of the area, you may have as good an insight into the future of your investment as any real estate agent.

Another example would be the collector of antiques who scours New England tag sales looking for the valuable piece of furniture or jewelry that a naïve owner is selling for next to nothing. A true find worth a great deal of money is certainly a rarity, but more modest values can be found by the aficionado of period collectibles for a fraction of their current worth.

Penny Stocks: Stocks selling at less than $2 a share. These stocks usually are in new companies with no track record to use as a guide to the company's performance. As with junk bonds, you would have some background information about the company's product or service that would help you recognize a new company with potential for growth and profit.

Now you have a comprehensive overview, illustrated in the following chart, of the kinds of investments available to you and the risk inherent in commonly offered products. But where do you buy these products? Recent changes in legislation have led to an ever increasing variety of vendors for financial products. It seems as if every commercial establishment—including your local supermarket—can provide you with some kind of financial service. In the next chapter, you'll find out who is offering what.

SPECTRUM OF INVESTMENTS

VERY CONSERVATIVE	CONSERVATIVE	MODERATE	MODERATE RISK	RISK
Certificates of Deposit	AAA-Rated Bonds	Corporate Zero Coupons	Growth Stocks	Junk Bonds
Treasury Bills	Tax-Free Bonds	Blue-Chip Stocks	Discount Bonds	Unappraised Tangibles
Savings Bonds	Government Bonds	Nonnuclear Utility, Bank, and Insurance Stocks	Tax Shelters	Penny Stocks
Money Market	Zero Coupons on CDs and Treasury Bills	Income-Focused Mutual Funds	Appraised Tangibles Social Investment Mutual Funds	

6
FINANCIAL STORES

All of the financial products listed in the last chapter are available to you through a variety of sources including banks, brokerage houses, and investment companies specializing in a specific financial product. In fact, recent legislation has broadened the services that can be provided by many financial institutions, so the lines between them are beginning to blur. Banks now offer investment advice. Brokerage houses offer checking accounts. Discount brokerage firms offer sales services without advice. On the one hand, your choice for financial counsel and sales services has never been greater. On the other, it has never been so confusing either. Where you decide to purchase your investment will be determined to a great extent, however, by what products you're interested in and what kind of guidance you require. Let's take a look at the "financial stores" open today and what they can offer you.

Banks: The stodgy old bank of last generation has been reoutfitted into a sophisticated financial institution that can offer you many financial and investment alternatives beyond checking and savings accounts. Most banks now offer a variety of credit card services. Many also offer investment opportunities in certificates of deposit, Treasury bills and Treasury bonds, and interest-bearing checking accounts including money market accounts that offer interest competitive with money market mutual funds. Some banks now have financial advisory services, too. Most also can help you set up a retirement account such as an Individual Retirement Account (IRA) or a Keogh Account for the self-employed customer. Though they can't offer trading services on the stock exchanges, some banks do offer mutual fund investment services. You can purchase shares in a mutual fund through your bank rather than through the mutual fund investment firm itself. And finally, some banks offer new computer access accounts that give you access to your money for most banking transactions other than cash withdrawals from your home.

As an added benefit to doing more of your financial business with your bank, most offer privileges to their most-valued customers who have a combination of several accounts, for example, an IRA, money market, and checking account. Common privileges include express service tellers, elimination of checking and service charges, and interest-rate reductions for certain loans.

What do all these new services mean to you, the customer? They mean that you have a choice. Rather than picking your bank because it's closest to your home or office, you should make your decision based on what services the banks in your community have to offer. Pick the one that will offer you the kind of financial support you need now and in the foreseeable future. More importantly, take the time to *use* the services offered to make your assets work hardest for you while costing you the least amount in service charges.

Brokerage Houses: Brokerage houses have been the traditional source of financial advice and investment services. Their services also have been expanded as a result of recent legislation making them capable of meeting all of your financial needs from checking and emergency lines of credit to credit or debit card needs to financial planning. The cost of the services offered by a brokerage house is covered by the commission paid on financial transactions handled by your broker.

A brokerage house provides you with a stockbroker who is both your financial advisor and your link to the greatest number of investment opportunities. Brokers can trade in stocks, bonds, options, Treasury bills, mutual funds (including money market funds), tax shelters, and commodities. No other financial institution offers that range of choice.

Many new investors have the impression that stockbrokers are only interested in large portfolios that will yield them large sales commissions. That's simply not the case today. So many financial opportunities are created today for the small investor to help him or her build financial security for tomorrow that an ever increasing percentage of many brokers' client load is young investors starting out with a few hundred dollars in an IRA or a starter investment account.

How do you pick a broker? Your first step is to look at the brokerage firm and what the firm can offer you in terms of financial support and services. Most brokerage firms will be happy to send you information on their services if you call and ask for it. Just as you would do when choosing a bank, you would choose your brokerage firm based on the services provided that meet your immediate and foreseeable future needs.

Once you've settled on one or two firms that interest you, you can call and set up an appointment to meet with a broker for an interview. Even if a friend recommends a broker to you, call and ask for an interview to make sure that you and the broker see eye to eye on the investment strategy you want to take. All brokers have their own investment philosophies. Some are more conservative than others; some more risk-oriented. You want to make sure that you and your broker share the same investment temperament so that you're not always at odds on financial decisions.

You also need to interview your broker to establish what kind of relationship you want with him or her. Keep in mind that there is no one right relationship in terms of making money. What makes a broker/client relationship right is each participant's ability to undertand each other and work together comfortably. Though each broker/client relationship is unique, most can be characterized in one of the following ways:

The Independent Investor: In the relationship with the independent investor, the broker mostly helps buy and sell investments that the client chooses him- or herself. The client also might ask the broker for some specific information about a potential investment, but the independent investor likes to make his or her own decisions on when, where, and how the money is invested. In this case, the broker's role as financial advisor is minimized. He or she carries out the financial plans devised by the investor.

This relationship is most often formed when the client takes on money management and investing as an avocation and spends a considerable amount of time doing the research into investments and following fluctuations in the economic climate that normally is part of the broker's job.

The Informed Investor: The informed investor depends on his or her broker to keep up to date on new financial products as well as to recommend investment strategies to take advantage of economic trends. However, this investor wants to read the background information on any investment before the broker actually makes a transaction. In this way, the investor is informed about what options he or she has and can make a choice among the investment suggestions offered by the broker, thus retaining some degree of control over his or her financial strategy.

The Dependent Investor: This investor either doesn't have the time or lacks the inclination to take an active role in choosing investments. While he or she will work out financial goals with the broker, the dependent investor expects the broker to choose and manage the investments to meet those goals.

Before you make a list of questions for a potential broker to answer during an interview, you should determine what kind of investor you are by asking yourself the following questions:

1. Are you more comfortable with conservative investments that offer you a steady, known amount of return than riskier investments that offer growth but a higher risk of capital loss?
2. Do you want to read background information on investment options your broker chooses for you and make your decision based on that information, or do you want the decision to be left in your broker's hands?
3. Do you want your broker to be available to offer you research and advice on investments you hear about independently?
4. Do you want to map out your financial goals and use your broker's advice to attain them, or do you want your broker to help you create a financial plan designed to make the most of your income?
5. Are there some investments to which you have an aversion?

When you've answered these questions, you'll have some idea what kind of investor you are, and you'll be able to ask meaningful questions during your interview that will reveal whether or not you and a potential broker make a suitable investment team. Your financial advisor should be someone who is sympathetic to your needs. If you are uninterested in developing a financial strategy and want to turn that over to a broker, you'll want to make sure that the broker is interested in giving detailed financial planning advice as well as investment advice. If you want to be a participant in your investment decisions, you want to make sure that your broker is one who enjoys working with as well as for clients. If you like gambling with a little of your money in some moderate-risk or risk investments, make sure that your broker isn't a dyed-in-the-wool conservative who would steer you clear of anything lacking a guarantee. And finally, if you don't believe in certain investments, you want to make sure that your broker will honor your decisions and work with you to build a portfolio using only the financial products with which you're comfortable.

In sum, you want to ask your potential financial advisor if he or she will be comfortable with your particular investor personality so that you can work together to build your future financial security. Similarly, you want to be comfortable with your broker's investor personality.

Of course your financial needs and your desire for active participation in managing your investment portfolio change over time. You may find that you outgrow a relationship with a broker and have to move your account if your financial perspective changes. You may also find that the brokerage firm you first choose doesn't offer you the kinds of services you need as you mature financially, and that you have to move your account for that reason. It's ideal, of course, to find one broker with whom you can do business your whole life, but it's also important to recognize when your financial advisor or your brokerage firm no longer is giving you the kind of service you require so that you can find a new advisor to keep your financial strategy on track.

Discount Brokerage Houses: A discount brokerage house offers sales services at a reduced sales commission from those charged by traditional brokerage houses. However, discount brokerage houses limit their services strictly to trading. They do not offer the variety of services that a traditional brokerage house does, such as financial planning advice, research into investments, checking and credit card services, or in-house investment packages. The services of a discount broker are most useful for independent investors who are knowledgeable in the financial field and are directing their own portfolios. These investors usually make their own decisions about where to invest their money and then can call on the discount broker to buy or sell a financial product. Discount brokers handle many financial products but focus on stocks and bonds.

Investment Firms: Investment firms are companies that use your money to invest in a variety of financial products. Firms that offer one or more mutual funds were discussed in the previous chapter (see *Mutual Funds*). This is one kind of investment firm. Other firms use the capital they raise from investors to fund tax shelters, or buy real estate or collectibles. To invest in these firms, you usually have to contact the company directly for literature. Some investment firms advertise their product in the financial pages. Your broker or accountant may know about smaller investment firms specializing in an investment you're particularly interested in, such as collectibles or real estate.

The following table gives you a quick guide to who sells what in the financial world.

Now you know what investments are available to you, how secure they are, and where you can buy them. You're ready to take the next step, which is to find out which financial products are the best investments for you, and how much money you should commit to the various products to address your personal needs.

FINANCIAL STORES

	BANKS	BROKERAGE HOUSE	DISCOUNT BROKERAGE HOUSE	INVESTMENT FIRMS
Stocks, Bonds Convertible Bonds Options Commodities	Some bonds	X	X	
Savings Bonds Certificates of Deposit	X	X		
T-Bills	X	X	X	
Mutual Funds	X	X		X
Real Estate				X
Tax Shelters		X		X
Tax-Advantaged (IRA, Keogh)	X	X	X	X
Tangibles				X
Other Services	Checking, savings money market accts. credit card financial advice loans	Credit cards, loans, checking accounts money market accounts financial advice		Appraisal of tangibles

7

THE INVESTMENT PYRAMID

In the previous chapters, you learned about what investments are available today and the risk inherent in individual products. What wasn't discussed was how increased or decreased risk should affect your investment choices. In the last generation, any risk was reason enough to avoid an investment, but as we discussed earlier, today's portfolio needs a certain amount of moderate-risk or risk investments to achieve greater growth or tax relief. The investment pyramid shown here is a tool used to help investors apportion their funds appropriately to investments of increasing risk. By using the framework, you can achieve an economic base of security while providing for future growth of your principal as well.

The pyramid is divided into five levels corresponding to five categories of investments. The categories—Level 1 (Very Conservative), Level 2 (Conservative), Level 3 (Moderate), Level 4 (Moderate Risk), and Level 5 (Risk)—are the same ones used in the spectrum of investments. You can use the guide to find detailed information about the investments listed in the pyramid levels.

Take a look at how the five categories shape up on the pyramid. You'll note that Level 1 (Very Conservative)—the category in which your principal is virtually guaranteed—is the foundation and the largest section of the structure. This is one level on the pyramid that everyone must invest in for security. Your emergency fund of three months' expenses goes in there as do any other liquid assets necessary for installment payments on loans or income tax quarterly estimates, for instance.

Levels 2, 3, 4, and 5, representing investments of increasing risk, decrease in proportion to the foundation. This is the classic structure for an investment portfolio. You invest smaller amounts of funds as the risk factor increases. Thus, even if you feel that you're in a position to invest a significant amount of money in Level 4 or

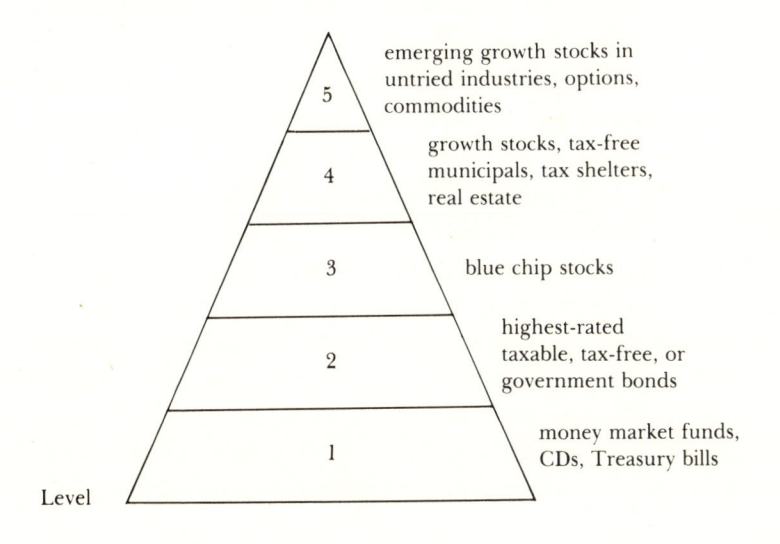

Level

5 — emerging growth stocks in untried industries, options, commodities

4 — growth stocks, tax-free municipals, tax shelters, real estate

3 — blue chip stocks

2 — highest-rated taxable, tax-free, or government bonds

1 — money market funds, CDs, Treasury bills

5, you'd still keep the majority of your funds in a combination of investments from Levels 1, 2, and 3 to provide for security. In general, you would never have more than 10 to 20 percent of your income tied up in Level 5 investments.

It's important to remember, however, that this pyramid is a point of reference, not the rule of thumb for investments. You might not use the precise proportions used in the pyramid for your investments. During the greatest income-producing years, for instance, it may be wiser to put half or more of available funds into Levels 3 and 4 and forego current income in return for later gains—as long as the foundation of liquid assets is available for emergencies. But as retirement nears, it's necessary to shift money out of growth investments aimed at increasing your principal and into securities that provide the greatest income while keeping your principal secure.

THE INVESTMENT QUIZ

The investment pyramid gives you a framework of proportions for your portfolio, but within that framework which specific investments are best for you? Most people think that the choice of investment is more of an emotional issue than anything else. Uncle Lewis invests in the market because he likes the gamble. Aunt Cynthia has put all of her savings into collectibles because she feels that she can always take them with her. Cousin Sarah only buys insured tax-free municipal bonds because she is risk-averse and averse to paying Uncle Sam as well.

While personal satisfaction with an investment is important, it is not the only factor dictating where your money should go. Your lifestyle, age, present and future financial commitments, as well as your investment temperament play a part in determining where you should put your money. All of those factors are taken into consideration in the investment placement quiz below. The quiz outlines which investment categories are best for you for your particular life circumstances. You'll find the answers to all of the questions in your personal financial profile.

Circle the answer that most nearly applies to you. If the question doesn't apply to you at all, leave the answer out. In the space at the right, write the number that appears in parentheses next to your answer.

My age is closest to:
(9) 30   (7) 40   (5) 50   (3) 60   (1) 70   _____

My present income (annual) from all sources is nearest
to (in thousands):
(2) 10   (4) 20   (5) 30   (6) 40   (8) 50   _____

In relation to income, my annual expenses approximate:
(1) 100%   (3) 90%   (5) 80%   (7) 70%   (9) 50%   _____

I presently have these dependents:
(9) 0   (8) 1   (6) 2–3   (4) 4–5   (1) 6 or more   _____

My assets, including house, insurance, savings,
and investments, total (in thousands):
(1) 50   (3) 100   (5) 250   (7) 350   (9) 500 or more   _____

My bills, mortgages, installment payments,
and debts in relation to assets approximate (in thousands):
(9) 30%   (7) 50%   (5) 75%   (3) 90%   (1) 100%   _____

I have cash on hand or other liquid assets to equal
this amount of expenses:
(1) 1 mo.   (3) 2 mos.   (5) 3 mos.   (7) 4 mos.   (9) 6+ mos.   _____

My life insurance coverage equals (in thousands):
(9) 250   (7) 150
(5) 100   (3) 50   (1) 25 or less   _____

My health insurance coverage includes:
(9) Basic, major medical, catastrophic
(5) Basic, major medical   (1) Basic   _____

Add up the numbers in the right column and divide by nine to get a median score. Then match your score to one of the numbers given below.

1. Insured savings accounts
2. High-grade government securities
3. High-quality corporate and municipal bonds, preferred stocks, unit trusts or mutual funds, and annuity income
4. Lower-rated corporate and municipal bonds, preferred stocks, investment trusts, convertible bonds and preferred stocks, and variable insurance
5. Higher-rated common stocks and investment trusts, investment annuities
6. Lower-rated common stocks and investment trusts
7. Speculative bonds, stocks, and investment trusts
8. Gold- and silver-related investments, foreign investment, foreign investment trusts
9. Rare and exotic investments: stamps, rare coins, art, antiques, gems and jewelry, rare books, autographs, prints and lithographs

Beside the number is a list of the investment areas that indicate the highest level of risk you can afford given your present financial circumstances. These scores are cumulative, however, so that your level includes not only the products listed next to the score, but all the investments listed previously as well. Thus, even someone with a score of nine should have some capital in the lower-level, more secure investments.

Another factor to keep in mind when you look at your score is your emotional comfort with risk. The higher your score the more *financially* able you are to absorb more risk. That doesn't necessarily imply that you are prepared emotionally for higher-risk investments, nor does it mean that you *must* take on such investments if you're uncomfortable with them. Remember, an investment strategy has to be both financially sound and emotionally attractive to be successful.

As mentioned above, the answer to this quiz reflects your current age and financial needs. As a result, it will change when significant events occur in your life. Therefore, a good way to keep up to date on your investment needs is to repeat the quiz whenever a major life change occurs, such as a change in jobs, marriage, the birth of a child, a promotion, and so on.

PUTTING IT ALL TOGETHER

Before you move on to the life-stage investment strategies in the next chapters, let's review the financial tools you have now and how they work together to help you take control of your financial future.

1. You filled out a *Personal Financial Profile* that helped you understand your current monetary situation as well as showed you ways in which you could change your situation to reach your goals.

2. You've become acquainted with the *Five Steps of money management* that will help you implement the financial changes you want to make for your different life stages.

3. You learned how to *follow key indicators* in the economic news, as well as how to look at general news from a financial angle. By keeping up with the news, you're becoming more aware of how the economic environment can affect your investment decisions.

4. You learned about the *basic investment categories*, what kind of return they pay and how you can track their performance in financial publications.

5. You learned about the *currently available financial products* in the major investment categories and how secure or risky they are.

6. You learned about the *investment pyramid* that showed you how your investment funds should be divided between secure and higher-risk financial products.

7. You learned what the *best investments* are for you given your current financial and personal circumstances.

The following examples of two people with different financial needs will show how these tools are used together to determine and act on a personal financial strategy.

Investor A finally sat down to work out her financial profile when she moved to a new firm and got a $5,000 raise in the transfer of which she kept $2,800 after taxes. She discovered that her credit card expenses were getting a little out of hand and decided to buy only what she could pay for at the end of the month rather than let small unpaid items mount up to big bills over several months. To make this decision feasible, she allocated $1,000 of her raise to additional spending for clothes, entertainment, cosmetics, and so on. The rest of the raise, she decided, would go to some investment program.

After reading the Five Steps, Investor A's first move was to get her $2,500 emergency money out of her income-bearing checking account which earned 5.5 percent interest and into a money market fund which earned 8 percent interest and might earn more if interest rates rose. Her next move was to open an IRA account at her bank and put $1,000 of her raise into that account this year. By contributing to an IRA and keeping track of her business expenses, she hoped to save money on her tax bill the following spring.

The $800 she had left over from her raise was the beginning of her investment fund. Investor A decided to put that money into a mutual fund that was growth-oriented but still within the moderate category of risk. She didn't need any income, but wanted her principal to grow in value as much as possible without sacrificing too much security. Once her investment fund had grown to $1,500, she planned to move her original $800 into a higher-risk investment that stood a chance of greater gains.

Investor B is in a different financial situation. He just completed his personal financial review to forecast what his financial situation will be when he retires in two years. His living expenses will be cut by a third when he moves out of his three-bedroom ranch house into a two-bedroom garden apartment. His tax status will also be lower once his regular income stops coming in. Even though he expects to earn a little money writing a monthly column for a professional trade magazine, he doesn't expect his income to provide for his day-to-day needs. Investor B, therefore, is looking to convert his assets from growth-oriented investments into secure, high-income investments that will preserve his retirement funds and give him a steady income. He knows from keeping up with the prevailing interest rates that he can lock in high interest rates in long-term corporate and government bonds now, and he wants to take advantage of the situation before interest rates fall as forecasted.

He has had a relationship with a broker for twenty years and is depending on her to advise him on the available products that will lock in the highest rate of return while providing the greatest security. The broker suggests a mutual fund that holds a portfolio of high-rated tax-free municipal bonds. This will provide a monthly or semi-annual income. She also suggests purchasing GNMAs ("Ginnie Mae's," or government agency bonds issued and guaranteed by the Government National Mortgage Association) which will also provide a steady monthly income. Thirdly, she suggests that he not think only of present income, but prepare for the future by investing in treasury zero coupons that will safely build up principal for later retirement years, perhaps ten years in the future.

If you were to break down the goals of these two people at opposite ends of their financial lives, you'd notice that they were working toward the same goals, essentially, which are the four basic investment objectives:

1. You want to make money.
2. You don't want to pay taxes.
3. You don't want to lose money.
4. You want liquidity.

However, the different immediate and future financial obligations of Investor A and Investor B lead them to reach their common goals through different investment strategies. Investor A, who has all the liquidity she needs and isn't in a high enough bracket to make taxes a major investment concern, is working toward building up her capital worth now. Investor B, who has met his capital appreciation needs, is working toward securing his worth as well as arranging a steady income that will be partially tax-advantaged or tax-free.

While the four basic investment goals are all important, one or another will dominate at various times in your life. Making money may be most important while you're a young adult. Making money and not paying taxes may be equally important during your middle years. Not losing money and liquidity may be most important in your later life.

Throughout your financial life, you need to know how to look critically at your portfolio and investment practices to make sure that your strategy is emphasizing the investment goal or goals dominating your current financial needs. For instance, you don't want to have your money tied up in financial products that are heavily taxed at a time when saving tax dollars is a major concern for you. You want to be aware enough to move your money into more tax-advantaged investments at that time so that you keep as much of your earnings as possible.

Flexibility within the framework of an investment strategy, then, is the key to success in financial planning. In the following chapters, you'll find a general guide to financial planning during two different life stages—early adulthood and middle age—that will show you how an active, flexible money management plan will allow you not only to meet the needs of these two life stages, but simultaneously will prepare you for the third life stage, retirement. Your needs may vary somewhat from those described here, but you will learn enough about adapting financial strategies to create a money management and investment plan tailored to your individual needs.

Part II

STARTING OUT: INVESTMENT STRATEGIES FOR AGES 25–45

8
GOALS FOR THE EARLY YEARS

You are part of the baby boom—that bulge in the population that defines styles and social trends as it moves from one age to the next. This generation of young adults is better endowed than any before, both in education and income potential. Most have a chance at more challenging and better-paying jobs than their parents, but even so, a large number are striking out on their own and creating a swell in the ranks of the small business owner. But whether he's working for himself or she's working for someone else, young professionals in this stage are a marketing manager's dream. They were brought up to expect the best, and they are willing to pay for it. They probably won't marry until their late twenties or early thirties, so they don't have any financial concerns other than their own comforts. Starting from scratch, they have to outfit themselves with furnishings, television, stereo, wardrobe, and video cassette recorder. Rather than save money on average-quality merchandise, young professionals are likely to research the product lines available and purchase the highest-quality item. By the time the young men and women in this stage of life settle down with a partner, they are each likely to have furnishings that their parents wouldn't have been able to afford until near retirement—if at all.

For all their educational sophistication and entrepreneurial spirit, most people in this age group have no real financial management experience. They undoubtedly will go through some rocky financial times in the twenty years ahead of them in this stage—sort of an economic adolescence. The hope is that the young adult not only will come into his or her own professionally at the end of this stage, but financially as well.

The goals of the young adult are often conflicting. For instance, when you're just starting your career, Dad says you should put some money away in case your job doesn't work out. But you've just seen a terrific deal on a sturdy second-hand car. The immediate need for transportation seems to outweigh the need for rainy-day security.

Then, when you're a newlywed, you start to put aside funds to buy an apartment. It will be the cornerstone of your family investments. The down payment is so enormous on property in one of the established neighborhoods, though, that it continues to elude you year after year. Five years later, you consider taking a chance on a new renovation in a marginal neighborhood. The price and financing will cost you half of that for an established cooperative apartment, but the risks to your investment are greater, too. Do the benefits of home ownership outweight the risks in this situation?

Another problem with financial management in this stage is the constant changing of circumstance and goals. One year you're single and earning next to nothing, the next you're engaged and earning twice what you were the year before. The reverse is also true. One year you're on top of your field, and the next you move on to another more challenging area of employment, but pay for it in a salary decrease. It often seems that before you've ironed out the conflicts you face in one situation, you're thrown into a new situation with entirely different goals and different conflicts.

ANTICIPATING CHANGING NEEDS

However your lifestyle changes during this tumultuous time, the Five Steps of personal money management will help you keep your financial planning on track. At this stage of life, during which you begin to accumulate some capital and also start to develop an economic base, the Five Steps provide a foundation for a lifelong money management plan.

STEP 1: MAXIMIZING YOUR LIQUIDITY.

When you're just starting out, you may not have much in the way of liquid assets to worry about. You may have just enough money to keep up with your monthly expenses. But in just a couple of years—maybe as a result of a promotion or a move to a different company—your income could become significantly larger than your expenses, and you'll be able to start setting aside your emergency fund of three months' expenses.

You don't want to have your accumulated funds from one paycheck to the next sitting in a checking account that doesn't pay interest. You may need to keep an average balance of $500 to $1,000 in your regular checking account to avoid monthly maintenance and check-writing fees, but any money above that balance is not working for you.

When you see your balance accumulating $300 and $400 a month, talk to your bank manager about upgrading your account to an interest-bearing product. Find out what the minimum balance is and what kind of interest is being offered. Then shop around at other banks for their interest-bearing accounts. Remember, banks are very competitive today. Services can vary considerably from one to another. By the time you've accumulated the usual minimum deposit for a money market account (about $2,500), you'll know where to go to get the highest interest and the best service for your money.

Don't make the mistake, however, of trying to increase the return on your emergency fund by putting it into a higher-paying six- or twelve-month certificate of deposit (CD). The difference in interest between the short-term CD and the money market account actually may be only a fraction of a percent and if you need your money in a hurry and have to liquidate your CD before it matures, you'll pay a penalty and forfeit some interest. You might even end up earning less interest on your CD because of the premature withdrawal than you would on the more liquid money market account in that case.

The moral here is not to be interest greedy. The wise investment choice is one that addresses all facets of your financial needs, not just the desire for high returns. Your emergency money should be available at any moment, and at the same time should be earning the highest rate of return available. However, you shouldn't sacrifice liquidity for a higher interest or you defeat the purpose of the emergency fund.

STEP 2: CONSOLIDATE ASSETS.

A young adult starting out often comes into some securities that were held in trust until he or she reaches age twenty-one, or some cash gifts upon graduating from college meant to ease the transition into financial independence. The contributions might be $1,000 in savings bonds from various aunts and uncles, one hundred shares of various stocks given for graduation from college, and perhaps a trust worth $5,000 from parents. As separate investments, these odd bits and pieces may not provide much of a financial base or direction for a young adult. However, in combination, these assets may provide that essential emergency fund of three months' expenses or a beginning investment portfolio.

Your first step in consolidating your assets is to look over what bonds, cash, or stocks you have and what your total worth is. Your parents may be able to help you with the figures if they've been overseeing your investments. You also can work out most of the figures yourself by looking up the bond and stock prices in the financial listings, adding their worth to any cash gifts you have.

Once you have an estimate of the cash value of your gifts, you can decide what you want to do with the money. You may decide to use all the cash as your emergency fund in which case you'd want it in a money market account either at your bank, with a mutual fund, or with a brokerage firm. On the other hand, you may decide to put part of it in a money market account and use the other part to begin building your assets.

If your decide to begin an investment portfolio, where's the best place to put your money? The specific answer to that question will depend on the financial climate at the time, your investment temperament, and your goals. Beginners often find mutual funds attractive because many have a low minimum investment while giving you the benefit of the returns on a large portfolio.

What kind of mutual fund is best for a beginner? There is no one answer to that question. You have to take into consideration what sectors of the financial market are prosperous at the time as well as what kind of investments interest you and what your goals for your money are. If you've noted an expansion in the stock market, you may want to put the money in a mutual fund that can take advantage of the active market, such as a growth stock fund. If the market is in a lull but interest rates are fairly high, you might decide to keep the money in a money market fund, a bond fund, or a utility stock fund in order to take advantage of the high interest rates. If you're not opposed to risk, you might put part of your money into an aggressive growth or international stock fund that aims for maximum capital growth but also has a higher risk of losses. At this stage in life, you can afford to risk a little loss for the chance of greater gains if you're comfortable with riskier investments.

Many firms offering mutual funds have a family of funds with varying financial goals and you can move your assets among the different funds to take advantage of economic and interest rate changes affecting your investments.

Mutual funds are not for everyone, however. If you want to make financial management an avocation and become active in trading individual stocks and bonds, you might benefit from starting out with the guidance of a broker or a financially experienced relative who can teach you how to piece together the information you gather from financial news sources in order to evaluate a certain sector of industry or a certain company.

If you go to a broker, be sure you make it understood that you want to direct your own investments so that you'll be given the research and information that you need. You might, for instance, feel that regional bank stocks look like a good investment given some recent news. You look in the corporate earnings reports in the daily financial papers for regional banks that look promising and then track the movement of their stocks for a week or so while you look over background information on the banks available from your broker. Then, you could go to your broker and ask if your intuition is on track before making the investment. In this kind of relationship, your broker can help you monitor the development of your investment skills to make sure that your judgment is sound, as well as give you access to many different kinds of information and research resources.

A third way for a beginner to handle consolidation is to choose a financial advisor or broker who will use his or her judgment to choose investment options suitable for your current financial condition and goals. In order for this relationship to work, you need to feel confident that your advisor is working with your investment temperament and financial welfare in mind. You should shop for your broker in the same way you would for a doctor. Get referrals from colleagues, friends, or relatives who have experience in this kind of relationship and then interview several financial advisors before turning your money over to an investment firm.

During the years of this stage of life, your income easily can double or even triple, and your early investments can grow into a substantial sum. You'll probably begin to accumulate a considerable amount of discretionary funds. At first, much of this money will go to upgrading your lifestyle. By the time you're in your mid-thirties, however, you probably will have acquired most of what you need to be physically comfortable. You may begin to feel that your beginner portfolio isn't broad enough to take advantage of the investment opportunities available to you given the increase in your discretionary funds. It may be time again to consolidate your assets, using the money to buy products that have more earning power, that provide you with some economic leverage, or that offer a tax advantage.

If you have $10,000 invested in a variety of conservative mutual funds, you might decide that some of that money might be better placed in a tax shelter (see "Step 4. Avoid Tax Shock"). A tax shelter is a higher-risk investment, but offers you a deduction in your tax bill and the possibility of future cash flow and/or capital gains. Your accountant may know of some quality tax shelters. A financial broker also will be able to help you find an attractive shelter or perhaps suggest another investment product being offered through the brokerage house that would suit your needs. Even if you've preferred to be an independent investor up to this point, you might want to engage a broker now for the areas of investment planning where research or access to the greatest variety of financial products is a priority. There's no law that says you can't mix a self-directed portfolio with one partially managed by a broker.

An example of a product available from many large brokerage firms that is useful for independent investors as well as for those who use the full services of a broker is the money management account. These accounts have a minimum initial deposit of $15,000, but that balance needn't be in cash. The deposit can be made up of a combination of cash—such as your three-month emergency fund—and various security holdings, or a combination of securities alone. You are in no way obligated to liquidate the investment on deposit. You just register them with the firm as part of your minimum deposit. The money management account acts as a repository for the securities. If you have $5,000 in emergency cash, for instance, and $10,000 worth of corporate bonds and stocks, you could consolidate your emergency money with your investment fund and have the initial deposit for a money management account.

For your deposit, you'd get the following services:

1. High interest on your cash deposit in a money market fund.

2. Check-writing privileges.

3. A debit card that could be used against a line of credit whose interest rate varies at a fixed amount over the prime interest rate. Any charges that you didn't pay at the end of the month would automatically be debited from your credit line. The interest rate charged on the credit line is usually lower than that charged by most major credit cards because it isn't fixed, but floats in relationship to the prime, so you would save finance charges.

4. A consolidated financial statement at the end of the month listing your account's opening and closing balance, detailed information about your check transactions (number and date of check as well as the person or establishment to whom the check was written), interest earned, line of credit used and interest charged, and the status of securities held in the account including price at the closing of the statement as well as dividends or interest paid. If you choose, you may also designate by code on your checks if the amount paid is a deductible expense. These encoded checks will be recorded separately in a section of your statement posting a monthly and year-to-date tally of your deductions.

5. The services of a financial advisor who could either manage your portfolio or act as the liaison between you and the marketplace.

The point to be made here again is that your financial needs may change dramatically during the transition from early to middle adulthood and you should periodically question your earlier financial decisions rather than follow the same investment pattern blindly year after year.

STEP 3: KNOW WHERE YOUR MONEY GOES.

Spending patterns in the early years of this life stage vary considerably from one year to the next. So many decisions about profession, location, marriage, and children are made, rethought, and made again that financial planning can only be transitory until some of these life-shaping forces are made permanent. Some of you may be treading water in a profession during your twenties until you finally get up the courage to break the cycle and return to school to begin a new career in your thirties. Others may move in with a prospective mate only to find two years later that you're not cut out to be a married couple. Still others might be enjoying a high-paying executive position that has to be forfeited to take on the demands of parenthood. Any of these milestone decisions can change your financial status overnight.

In the early years of this life stage, then, it's important to keep your finances as flexible as possible so that you can adjust for opportunities or unexpected changes. One way to manage fiscal flexibility is to be aware of how you're spending your money so that you can shift financial gears quickly if you need to. Maybe you're allowing yourself the luxuries of a car in the city, summer rental shares, and subscriptions to theater clubs or concert halls. There's no reason not to enjoy these when you're financially able, but if you suddenly lose a part of your salary due to a career change or a change in lifestyle, you should know where the luxuries in your budget are so that they can be trimmed.

Aside from your overview of spending patterns, you should also have a detailed record of expenses in order to segregate the tax-deductible from the non-tax-deductible. As mentioned before, this record can be a shoebox full of checks and charge account receipts that you sort out at the end of the year, or, if you have a money management account, your monthly financial statements. No sophisticated filing is necessary. You just want to make sure that you don't pay taxes on income when it's not necessary.

STEP 4: AVOID TAX SHOCK.
Tax-planning strategies might not be of much concern in the earlier years of this stage, but once you start earning $30,000 and more as a single taxpayer, or $50,000 as a two-career couple, you're going

to need to reduce your taxes in order to avoid a tax bill on top of your withholding at the end of the year.

Your first step is to tally up the deductible expenses you've been tracking throughout the year and figure out whether or not they can save you some tax dollars if you list your deductions on a long tax form rather than file the short form. If you use an accountant, he or she can tell you which form would be to your advantage after looking over your records.

Several tax-advantaged investments also are available to reduce your taxable income. One of the most popular is the Individual Retirement Account (IRA) that shelters up to $2,000 of income from taxes annually per working person. Also, income and capital gains earned in the IRA are tax-deferred until you start taking money out of the account. The only drawback is that this money is locked up until you're 59.5 years old, and you can't get to it—barring a disabling disease or injury—without paying a penalty. Thus, you wouldn't want to deposit any money in an IRA that you would need before that age.

Another investment that shelters income is the retirement funds set up by many employers. These act in the same way as an IRA—you don't pay taxes on the contribution or the income earned on the account. The difference lies in the amount of contribution you can make, and perhaps a benefit of matching funds scheduled by the company whereby they will match a certain percentage of your contribution.

Usually the company sets a lower limit, say 3 percent of your salary or a set dollar amount, that often adds up to more than your total IRA contribution allowance. The contribution is deducted from your paycheck automatically, so you can see the benefits of your tax planning immediately. Up to 50 percent of the contribution can come out of your tax bill, so you'll probably notice that the deduction from your paycheck only reflects as little as 50 percent of the contribution.

As mentioned earlier, once you have built up discretionary funds that can be used for longer-term planning, you might want to invest in a tax shelter that will bring you several years of tax benefits plus the opportunity for capital gain or income in years to come. Public limited partnerships are popular with smaller investors. These shelters, usually offered through a brokerage house, can be bought into for as little as $5,000. The lifetime of these public limited partnerships averages seven to ten years. During the early years, you usually receive a write-off on your tax return. At the same time, you may begin receiving cash flow from the investment that sometimes is sheltered from taxes. The final goal of the investment, however, is long-term capital gain at the end of the partnership's life when you receive back your initial investment plus an estimated return on the principal.

Privately placed tax shelters, also sold through brokerage firms or by companies that specialize in raising funds for tax-sheltered investments, usually require a much higher initial investment than a publicly offered shelter. Investments may start at $50,000 and scale higher. In some of the privately placed tax shelters requiring larger investments, the contributions are broken up into payments over three to five years. The periodic payments are substantial, as are the anticipated benefits of the tax shelter. These investments really are only for the big salary earner or someone who has recorded a windfall year. Your accountant or broker can give you advice on which shelters look most attractive, and which are appropriate for your income level.

Tax planning also comes into the choice of investment you make. When you get into a bracket where you're giving up a third to a half of your income—such as from interest and dividends—to the government, you might want to reinvest your money in products whose returns are partially or wholly tax-free. A money market fund or a municipal bond mutual fund, for instance, can be limited to investments in tax-free bonds, making the interest earned federally tax-free and sometimes state and locally exempt. Individual tax-free bonds or municipal bonds also might be a good place to put some of your investment funds. Some of you might look at these tax-exempt bonds and be concerned about the lower rate of return compared to taxable investments such as CDs. However, when you consider the tax bite taken out of taxable returns, these untaxed investments can seem quite attractive. You can determine whether or not tax-exempt investments will increase your return by calculating the difference between your earnings on similar taxable and exempt products.

For example, let's say that you can earn 9.5 percent on your money market account at the bank. A tax-free money market fund offered through a mutual fund or through your brokerage house may offer you 6.0 percent interest. Does it make sense to move your funds into the tax-free account? It certainly does if you're in the 50 percent bracket. You'd only keep 4.75 percent of your interest with the taxed money market account. However, if you are in the 33 percent bracket, you'd be keeping 6.3 percent of the interest on the taxed money market account, which is higher than the 6.0 percent tax-free interest.

MONEY MARKET	50% BRACKET	33% BRACKET
Tax-Free 6%	6%	6%
Taxable 9.5%	4.75%	6.3%

Tax-advantaged and tax-exempt investments are an important part of a portfolio, but you shouldn't go overboard with them, choosing all of your investments based on the taxes they'll save you. Your portfolio needs to be balanced between quality stocks offering the potential for long-term capital gains (the increase on investments sold after at least six months and one day that are taxed at a lower rate than short-term gains), short-term, liquid investments paying the highest yield while providing you immediate access to your emergency funds, and tax-advantaged investments aimed at keeping your tax bill as low as reasonably possible.

STEP 5: PLAN FOR SHORT-TERM AND LONG-TERM FINANCIAL NEEDS.

When you start your first job, the future seems to encompass the next six months at the most. However, it's at this tenuous position in your independent financial life that you need the security of an emergency fund the most. So short-term financial planning in the form of building an emergency fund as quickly as possible is essential. Putting away money for a rainy day is particularly hard when that money almost always comes out of discretionary income used for entertainment and travel, but it's critical to your financial security. You never want to be at the mercy of a job or a relationship because you don't have the money to support yourself while you break the old ties and move on to something else. Instead of disaster money, think of your emergency cash as a freedom fund that will give you three months without financial worry to redirect yourself to a better future.

Once you find a position you like and a place to set down roots, you might start looking ahead to future needs like buying a home, a car, or furthering your education. Financing for major expenses can be arranged in a number of ways, not necessarily the best of which is saving and then spending the lump sum you need. It might be more to your advantage to use your savings or investment portfolio as leverage to get a low-interest loan. The loan will pay for the tuition or the down payment on the car or house, and the principal will still be able to grow and accrue dividends or interest.

For instance, let's say that you need a car. The financing you can get from the dealer or the bank is running close to 14 percent. What options would you have? One might be to use the credit line connected to your money management account, if you have one. The interest might be lower on the credit line than on the bank loan because the interest on the credit line floats only a couple of points above the prime rate. Another might be to use an investment as collateral to secure a loan. Loans secured by collateral, such as stocks or bonds, often carry lower interest charges than unsecured loans. For instance, if you owned shares in a utility stock and habitually reinvested the dividend payments, you might decide to use the stock and the reinvested dividends to secure your loan. To make the loan even less of a burden, you might apply your quarterly dividend payments toward your car payments directly rather than reinvesting them. When your loan was paid up, you would still have your investment and you could return to your past habit of reinvesting the dividends.

Future planning shouldn't always center around spending money. Investing for long-term capital gains also needs to be a part of your long-term financial strategy. In this age group, your choice of investment products is not constrained by the concerns of later life stages, when income may become a primary objective as a result of increasing financial obligations. Most of your investment funds can be put into the moderate or moderate-risk categories—growth stocks and tax-advantaged investments (e.g., IRAs, company retirement funds, municipal bonds, tax shelters). You won't see much in the way of income, but you will be in a position to see your principal greatly increase in value. For this goal, you want to look for long-term capital gain in a solid stock situation. This kind of investment can increase your net worth while diminishing your future tax bill on the capital growth, because the long-term investments will fall under the long-term capital gains tax, which is substantially lower than short-term gain, interest, or ordinary income tax.

One financial product you probably would not want to buy during the early years of this stage is life insurance. Many people in the mid- to late-twenties today are single taxpayers. An investment in life insurance won't provide them with a tax advantage as their earning power increases, and they have neither a spouse nor children to protect—the primary reason for purchasing life insurance. Under normal circumstances, the insurance provided as a benefit by most employers is adequate.

As you can see from the suggestions in this chapter, the young adult is usually subjected to a bombardment of life changes that requires a reworking of financial underpinnings. On account of the chaotic nature of these years, you won't find hard and fast rules on money management for the age group twenty-five to forty-five. The hallmarks of a successful financial plan at this time are flexibility and frequent review. Keep your management habits current with your lifestyle. Don't get stuck in an economic rut that is irrelevant to your present needs.

Ages 25–45: GOALS
- Build 3-month emergency fund
- Build personal wealth
    —Invest in long-term securities with moderate risk and promise of substantial capital gain
- Lower taxes
    —Contribute to IRA and other retirement funds for tax deduction and future security
    —Invest in tax-advantaged products including tax shelters and tax-free bonds
    —Keep track of tax-deductible expenses

9
HANDLING TWO INCOMES

In our parents' generation, the two-income household was the exception, and the household with two equal incomes was a rarity indeed. Today, however, economic pressures as well as recent social changes make the household with two equal incomes part of a new economic tradition. For instance, a growing number of women and men are remaining single through their twenties and even into their early thirties. Instead of working out the economics of a couple's budget, these single people often find themselves enmeshed in the financial problems of sharing household expenses with a roommate. And when these young adults do marry, their economic picture is often the antithesis of their parents'. Where most of our mothers worked only until they married, today's bride is likely to be a career woman with more than five years experience behind her and no intention of leaving her job on her wedding day. She often comes into the marriage with as much equity as her husband, so the questions of what is ours and what is mine become complicated and uncomfortable. In either case, we have few role models to use as guides for money management during these early adult years. Too often we have to resort to summer-camp tactics: labeling our belongings—even our food—with masking tape. Well, that didn't work at camp, and it doesn't work at home either.

ROOMMATE ECONOMICS

The finances of single working roommates are significantly different than those of school roommates. Costs of students living together often can be fairly evenly divided, but the household budgets and needs of young professionals can vary considerably depending on lifestyles and business-related expenses.

Roommates need to sit down when they move in together and figure out what their common living expenses are and how they are going to break them down. Some roommates have similar enough schedules and tastes that they can contribute equally to a weekly food bill and share shopping responsibilities. Other roommates find their eating habits so different that they each end up with separate food bills for the week. However, they do share household basics like soap, shampoo, detergent, and other cleaning items. Rather than rely on memory to determine whose turn it is to buy what, it's wise to do a monthly shopping for these goods and split the bill at that time.

The deductible and/or reimbursible expenses of professionals also differ, and these variables should also be taken into consideration when costs are broken down. For instance, if one roommate's firm covers the basic phone costs at home because of the extensive use of the home phone for business, then that roommate should consider paying all of these phone costs rather than splitting them because she'll be reimbursed for them. If magazine subscriptions are a deductible item for one roommate, then it makes sense for him to cover the whole cost in order to get the tax advantage.

Another major consideration of roommates is how to handle

home purchases. Whether or not you split the ownership of household furnishings will depend on how you would handle dividing up the household if one roommate moved. Would you each want the option to buy out the other roommate in order to keep the household intact while giving the departing person a fund to refurbish his new home? In that case, sharing the cost of buying furniture, linens, and home entertainment products would make sense. However, if you prefer to know that the investments you made would be permanently yours to move from one home to the next, it would be more appropriate for each roommate to make individual purchases to contribute to the apartment.

An extremely important part of roommate economics is making sure that you have a contingency fund to pay the whole rent in case your roommate or roommates move out at a time when you want to continue living in the apartment. You may be lucky and find replacements for the people who leave before you're faced with covering extra rent. However, you don't want to be forced into accepting a roommate who might not be right for you because you don't have the funds to cover extra rent for a month or two. If you pay only part of a monthly rent, then it might be wise to increase your three-month emergency fund to include three months' full rent as opposed to just your share.

OWNING WHAT YOU SHARE

In the last generation, marriage followed closely after school, so questions of significant investment rarely came up for single individuals. Today, however, young professionals often push off marriage while establishing their careers. Many single professionals are in a financial position where they can—and should—make sizable investments with their disposable income to increase their worth. One way to split the risk and lower cost of large investments, such as real estate, is to go in on it with someone else. It's not uncommon anymore, for instance, for roommates to buy an apartment rather than rent one. Individuals who rent summer shares regularly may also decide to invest in a piece of property in the area and own their shares rather than rent them every year.

Sharing ownership of property with a fellow occupant can work out fine if the partners agree on the terms of ownership. For instance, you might want to make a condition that if one partner has to move, the investment should be liquidated at market value so that each of you gets your share back and can be free to use the money in another venture. This may be the most clear cut way of handling an unforeseen move, but it may force a premature sale of the property. To avoid having to sell the house or apartment before it reached maximum value, you could make arrangements for either one partner to buy out the other at current market value, or for either partner to rent his or her part of the property to cover mortgage, tax, and maintenance costs until a more favorable time for sale of the property occurs. However you decide to handle the unexpected departure of your partner and roommate, make sure that the solution is agreeable to both investors and that it is written down as part of the obligation between you.

When jointly owning property with a roommate, you also have to address who will inherit the property in the event of your death. Basically, you can handle your investment in two ways. If you are joint tenants with your roommate, you jointly own the property, but if something happens to you, your share will go to some other party. If, however, you are joint tenants with rights of survivorship, the property only changes hands between the two of you. If something happens to you, your roommate inherits your share of the house. If something happens to your roommate, you inherit his or her share.

MARRIAGE AND MONEY

When Sharon, a thirty-two-year-old word processor, and Michael, a thirty-year-old news cameraman, decided to marry, they set their wedding date, picked out rings, decided on a traditional Protestant marriage and an outdoor buffet at Sharon's parents' house after the ceremony, and then sat down with their lawyer to draw up a prenuptial financial agreement. Sharon and Michael didn't see that last step as a contradiction of their other actions. To them, a prenuptial agreement simply made sense. They had both built up assets before they were married, and they wanted to record what their individual worth was just in case their marriage didn't work out as they had planned. The couple knew contemporaries whose early marriages had ended in divorce. Divorce was not the unthinkable thing that it was to their parents. It was a fact of life.

Sharon and Michael are starting out their joint finances on the right foot. Many people view prenuptial agreements as the sign of a weak commitment to the marriage vows. Instead, they are an economic and legal necessity given today's changing divorce laws and dual-income households. Try to think of the prenuptial agreement as you would life insurance or a will—as a financial guideline to be used in the event of an unforeseen tragedy. If working out actual guidelines for separation of finances is too uncomfortable, you can do what Sharon and Michael did—just list both partners' individual assets at the time of the marriage.

With your prenuptial agreement out of the way, you can put your mind on the wedding day. It's a day not only of great personal importance, but financial significance as well. Most couples today, like Sharon and Michael, will have two incomes. They will undoubtedly be catapulted into a higher tax bracket once they start filing a joint return. One factor that will affect their ability to lower their first tax bill is the date on which they are married. If they pick a day in the first half of the year, they'll have a few months to invest in some tax-advantaged or tax-sheltered products that will protect their income from bracket creep. Of course, some wedding dates are chosen for sentimental reasons, but many are set to take advantage of good weather or a wide range of honeymoon choices. Doesn't it make sense to consider financially auspicious dates as well? With such forethought, you might even find that you have more money to spend on a perfect honeymoon.

Once the wedding is over, the newlyweds will find themselves in a whole new financial arena with many more opportunities open to them because of their combined assets. Of course, their needs and future planning will change too, and a new financial strategy must be set.

Marriage is one of the life events that necessitates a review of personal finances from the ground up. You need to start out with a Personal Financial Profile that will reflect your combined income, new rent or mortgage expenses if you have them, combined assets, and combined liabilities. The new review will give you a reference to use when you reexamine the basic Five Steps of money management to make sure that your financial positioning is still the most advantageous it can be now that you're a two-income family. Let's look at how the strategies to achieve the goals of the five steps can change when you become a two-income household.

THE FIVE STEPS TO MANAGING YOUR MONEY

STEP 1: MAXIMIZE YOUR LIQUIDITY.

You can start taking advantage of your new marital status by combining your liquid assets into one account. If you combine the balances from your money market or checking accounts and add in your three-month emergency funds, you're likely to have the minimum balance necessary to open a money management account with a brokerage firm. You'll not only be earning high interest, but you'll be gaining the expertise of a broker to help you plan for the future.

A money management account can also help a married couple avoid arguments centered on who is keeping tabs on the checking account. When both partners are poor financial managers, the checkbook can be a source of frequent confrontations: Who forgot to enter a check in the book? Who bounced a check? Who forgot to pay last month's credit card bills? Who has been using the funds set aside for emergencies? A money management account would take care of much of the routine bookkeeping and financial managing for you. For instance, you can instruct your broker to take out a predetermined amount of money automatically each month from your money market checking account funds and put it into a longer-term, higher-yielding, or tax-advantaged investment. There it will not be subject to erosion as might occur in a more accessible checking account. You'll also have your major credit card expenses deducted from your liquid funds immediately. If the expenses go beyond your ready cash, your broker will be able to tap an automatic, low-interest line of credit for the balance of the payment. You'll have to enter your checks in your checkbook as you go along, but reconciling your checkbook to your statement will be easier because the financial statement you receive at the end of the month not only lists the number and amount of each check, but also the person or establishment to whom the check was written. Any check entries missing from your record can be identified easily. Finally, through the use of a simple code on your checks, your money management brokerage account statement can show your year-to-date tax deductions every month.

Of course, you don't need a money management account to take advantage of high interest rates. You could also use part of your emergency money to make the minimum deposit into a money market account offered by your bank that might entitle you to free checking and other banking privileges. Check with your banker to see what programs are offered when you combine a high interest-bearing account with your regular checking account.

The rest of your combined liquid assets could go into a money market mutual fund that may offer higher interest rates than your bank along with some limited checking privileges.

Couples who do keep their money in several accounts should

elect one partner to oversee the maintenance of the bank books. Sharing the job almost always results in confusion. Both partners always want to know who was responsible for balancing the books last month, or who wrote the check whose number is missing from the record, or why the balance went below the minimum in the preceding two months and caused them to lose their interest advantage. You can see where sharing the checkbook duty can become a major battleground for newlyweds.

Some partners, used to managing their money individually, prefer to keep separate checking accounts and pay a part of the household expenses proportional to their salaries. Even if this is the way you prefer to handle your two incomes, you still should consider combining your emergency money funds in order to meet the minimum deposit requirements on the highest-interest-earning money market fund available.

STEP 2: CONSOLIDATE ASSETS.

Marriage may be a time of spiritual joining, but it shouldn't be a time of complete financial consolidation. While combining liquid assets as discussed previously is desirable, separation of other assets can be more beneficial than consolidation because of the way that estate tax laws are constructed currently. Today the government allows the surviving spouse an unlimited deduction on estate taxes associated with the deceased partner's assets. Keep in mind that the deduction is applied to the *appreciated value* of the assets, not the value at which the assets were initially purchased. Therefore, you would not have to pay estate taxes on the principal or on the capital appreciation of any securities, valuables, or property willed to you if the investments were in your partner's name alone. However, if you owned all of your assets jointly, your deceased spouse's half of the investment would be exempt from tax, but your half would not. Thus, you wouldn't have to pay taxes on your spouse's half of the capital appreciation of an asset, but you'd have to pay taxes on your half. Let's look at an example of how this concept works.

A and B jointly bought $1,000 worth of a stock ten years ago in both of their names. Today that investment is worth $3,000. If A were to die, her half of the initial investment ($500) plus her half of the profit on the investment ($1,000) would be inherited by B tax free. Thus, if B liquidated the investment, the half of the profit belonging to A's estate would be tax-exempt, but the $1,000 belonging to B would be taxable at the regular rate.

If, however, A had purchased the $1,000 of stock in her name only, B would have inherited the entire appreciated value of investment ($3,000) under the unlimited marital deduction. Thus, the full $2,000 profit would have been exempt from tax.

Of course if you keep your assets under different names, you need a will drawn up that designates your spouse as the beneficiary of your estate and specifies any other gifts or bequests you wish to make. Too many young couples feel that a will is something to draw up when you're on your death bed. On the contrary, you need a will any time you've acquired valuable assets in order to make sure that your estate is handled as you would want it to be, and that your assets go where you intend them to.

STEP 3: KNOW WHERE YOUR MONEY GOES.

A critical step in creating a successful financial plan for two people is finding out how each feels the household money should be spent. Does one partner put every unassigned dollar into a money market account? Does the other like to save a set amount and then spend the rest of his income as he sees fit? Does one like to spend money on household furnishings while the other prefers to keep up subscriptions to the symphony and dine at her favorite French restaurant once a week?

Newlyweds need to sit down and find out what each partner needs from the household income to feel satisfied. Undoubtedly, the newlyweds' budget will not be able to accommodate the financial habits of both partners prior to their marriage. And undoubtedly, each partner will feel that his or hers is the more important expense. The only way to avoid long, unproductive battles over money is to allow some room in the budget for both partners' needs. Compromises have to be made about how much money will be saved, how much spent on a new car, and how much used for discretionary income, but husband and wife should come away from budget negotiations with their most important financial habits supported.

One way to approach these financial negotiations is for each partner to sit down and make a pie chart of his or her budget that indicates how his or her income is ideally spent in a given month. Here are two sample charts:

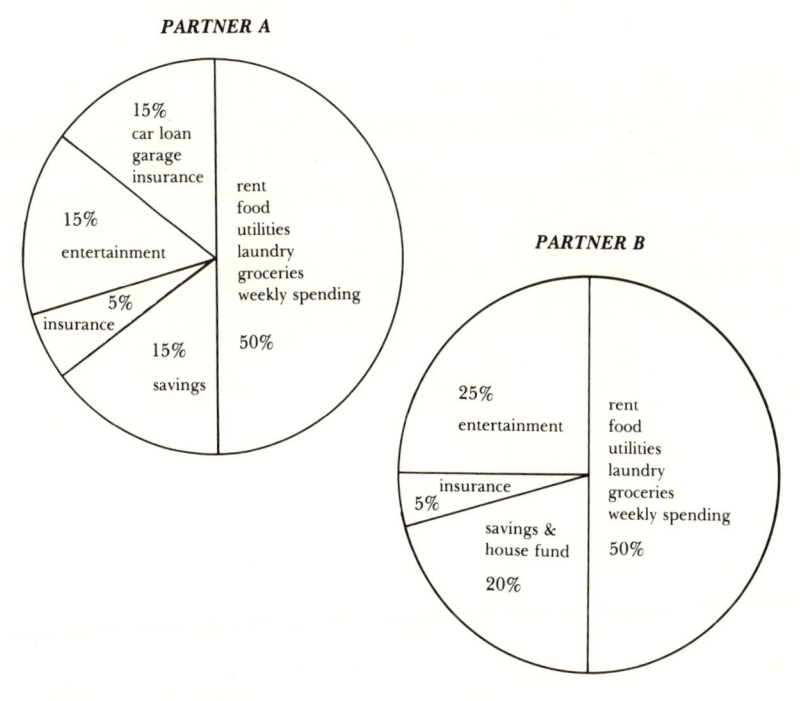

PARTNER A

- 15% car loan garage insurance
- 15% entertainment
- 5% insurance
- 15% savings
- 50% rent food utilities laundry groceries weekly spending

PARTNER B

- 25% entertainment
- 5% insurance
- 20% savings & house fund
- 50% rent food utilities laundry groceries weekly spending

Partners A and B aren't that far away from each other in terms of financial philosophy. Each has entertainment, savings, and necessity money outlined. However, A wants a car and B doesn't. He, instead, wants to put part of the car money toward more theater subscriptions and a vacation home fund. Rather than locking horns and battling back and forth, A and B could look for a way to compromise that will lead to both people getting part of what they want. B could suggest that A lower the cost of the car by purchasing a less expensive model this first time and parking on the street instead of in a garage, except when necessary. That would bring her costs down to 10 percent of their monthly income. A could suggest that B split the 5 percent of their monthly income left over between greater entertainment expenses and a vacation house fund, and also apply a small percentage of their savings annually to the vacation home fund to build it more rapidly.

Of course, it is not always so easy to reach a compromise. Sometimes both partners need to forfeit something they want or have had while single to reach a financial agreement. The pie chart at least will help newlyweds see what is economically feasible and what is out of their reach so that they can plan their spending realistically.

STEP 4: AVOID TAX SHOCK.

A primary concern of two-income households is to lower taxes where possible. Often the investment strategies of a single person no longer make sense when he or she marries. Almost certainly, the two incomes now joined in the same tax return will push the newlyweds into a higher tax bracket. Tax-advantaged and tax-sheltered investments that may not have made sense to each partner on his or her own now become important parts of financial planning. For instance, perhaps putting liquid assets into a tax-free money fund didn't make any sense when you were single and in the 33 percent bracket. You could earn 6 percent in the tax-free money fund, but after taxes, you could take home 6.6 percent in the taxable money fund earning 9.5 percent. Now, however, your two incomes put you in the 45 percent bracket and a tax-free money fund might help you keep more of your interest every year.

Another way to take income out of the present tax year is to put short-term investment funds—money that you need in six to nine months—into six- or nine-month certificates of deposit or Treasury bills. While interest in savings, money market accounts, and interest-bearing checking accounts is paid and taxed daily, interest on CDs and Treasury bills is taxed only at maturity when it is received and credited. The postponement of the reported interest may push that income into the following tax year when your tax bill might be lower because of tax-sheltered investing, a change in the household income or even a revision of federal tax laws.

Newlyweds might also consider transferring long-term investments into tax-advantaged investments such as tax-free mutual funds or municipal bonds. What about a publicly offered tax shelter? Maybe this is the time to consider getting into one to reduce your annual tax bill as well as build your future capital worth. Minimum investments in publicly offered tax shelters range from $3,000 to $5,000, so you shouldn't automatically consider these investments out of your reach.

If you or your spouse has a retirement plan, such as an employee benefits plan, take advantage of this tax-saving device after consulting a tax advisor. Usually, these plans are funded by a portion of your salary, some or all of which is deducted before taxes. The adjustment to your withholding taxes is made immediately, so you get the benefit of your lowered tax bill in every paycheck.

If you are already contributing to an employee plan, reconsider your annual contribution in the light of your new dual-income household. Could one or both of you afford to put a greater percentage of pretax income into the accounts? By doing so, you might be able to bring your income down into a lower bracket so that you save doubly on taxes because you get the deduction from your salary, and the remaining income may be taxed at a lower rate overall if it falls into a lower tax bracket.

Another tax-advantaged investment available to couples is the Individual Retirement Account, which allows each partner to make an annual tax-deductible contribution into a retirement fund. Even if you both have a retirement plan at work that allows for annual tax-deductible contributions of a certain percentage of your salaries, you can still open IRAs.

IRAs are not only attractive because they are a tax deduction available to every working person in the country, but also because the annual contribution can be any amount up to $2,000 per working person per year, or up to $2,250 per couple with one nonworking spouse. (The latter amount is likely to increase in the near future.) The flexibility in contribution allows for fluctuations in your joint income from one year to the next, which is important for married couples in this age group when children are born and career changes are common. Each year you can alter your contribution to match your tax needs. You can even skip a contribution if you need to.

Because IRAs are intended to fund your pension years, many couples in the early years of this life stage feel that the investment is inappropriate for them when their financial needs are more immediate. However, when considered as a tax-savings device, the benefit of this investment for young couples becomes apparent. A couple whose joint income is in the 33 percent bracket would save $1,320 on their tax bill by contributing the maximum $4,000 annually to their IRAs.

All of the investment options given previously can help you save on your dual-income tax bill. However, to maximize the effectiveness of your tax-reduction planning, you and your partner need to review your income and tax status with an accountant or investment advisor to determine how much of your money needs to be in tax-advantaged investments as well as which investments you and your partner find most advantageous.

STEP 5: PLAN FOR SHORT-TERM AND LONG-TERM FINANCIAL NEEDS.

Though a couple may be able to buy small items, such as records, books, or a case of a favorite wine, without consulting one another, any sizable purchase requires that both partners agree on a price range and a means of acquiring the funds for the purchase. Planning for major expenses can be the cause of friction in many marriages. The key to avoiding marital mayhem is to let each partner decide on a priority and then make short-term financial plans that work toward both goals. If you want a new stereo system and your spouse wants a motorcycle, establish a plan to raise the money for both, with each partner putting in $50 or $100 a week. Or, if there's some time limit on one purchase but not on another, put all of the funds toward the one expense and then keep the same savings mechanism active until the second purchase can be made.

Another way to approach short-term planning is to look at what assets you have that can be used as leverage to get the financing you need at a low cost. Money management accounts were mentioned earlier as a source of low-cost credit. Another place to get short-term funding is from a home equity loan. However, because the bank can take possession of your home should you default on such a loan, you'd want to be sure that you can meet the monthly payments for the length of the loan. You can also use your assets, such as stocks or bonds, as collateral for a loan. A secured loan, one backed by collateral, may cost you less in interest than an unsecured loan.

There may be more options open to you for short-term financing needs depending on your bank or broker's financing programs. The important point to remember here is to be creative when you think about financing something you want and talk to several sources before committing yourself to any financial plan.

Long-term financial plans can be just as problematic for a couple as short-term objectives. One person wants to salt away every spare penny and the other wants to use a good part of what is made during the early years to make life more enjoyable. One way to settle this typical argument is to contribute annually the full allowable amount to two IRAs. Instead of arguing about how much you need to put away to be prepared for the future, settle in the meantime on the IRA contributions as your target. The spouse who wants to upgrade her lifestyle can't argue with the amount because the contribution is made up in good part out of tax dollars that would have gone to the government if they weren't reclaimed through the deductible expense. The spouse who wants to build a safe future today will also be satisfied because the IRA offers him the opportunity of tax-deferred earnings that will make his money grow faster than it would if it were in a taxable investment. For instance, if you're in the 33 percent tax bracket and invest $2,000 annually in an IRA for twenty years at an interest rate of 10 percent a year that is tax-deferred, your $40,000 total investment will end up being worth $114,500. If you made that same $2,000 annual investment for twenty years into a taxable security, you would only have $79,000 for your $40,000 investment.

A second common disagreement between partners is what to do with the money they set aside for the future. It's important for a couple to realize that there's no one "right" way to invest money to secure your future. Some people who like to keep a good part of their funds in moderate-risk to risk investments can win more than they lose and end up with sizable funds for college tuitions, retirement, or whatever else they may need in the future. However, other investors who prefer to lock in high rates of return over fifteen to twenty years also achieve their future financial goals without all of the stress of watching volatile investments skyrocket one day and plummet the next.

What you might want to do if you and your partner can't see eye to eye on all your investments is to allow each spouse to control his or her IRA investment strategy. In this way, the more conservative partner will be able to put money into government bonds and government zero coupons while the partner who looks for a little more excitement in investing will have a chance to put money in an aggressive growth mutual fund or other more speculative investments that, while not insuring steady income, provide a chance for greater capital growth.

For couples who are undecided about where to put the money to make the most of their long-term funds, here's a rule of thumb for your portfolio: Divide up your assets proportionately between conservative, moderate, moderate-risk, and risk investments so that 40 percent of your cash goes into conservative investments, 25 percent into moderate, 25 to moderate-risk, and 10 into risk. In this age group, you can afford to take a chance with the higher-risk investments that will offer you a chance at the greatest gains.

However you decide to handle the economic issues in your marriage, try to keep in mind that most people bring definite ideas about money to a relationship. They might not be interested in the details of management, but they have overall fears and beliefs that have to be addressed if a family financial plan is going to work. If your husband needs insured tax-free bond certificates in his safe-deposit box to feel secure, let him have them. But remind him that they are not creating equity in a financial management account that way. If your wife likes to gamble on young companies, work out a budget for her speculative urges. Remember that there's room for every kind of investment in a financial plan. You *need* diversity to achieve your economic goals.

Goals for two-income households:
- **Lower taxes through tax-advantaged investing:**
  1. **IRA, retirement programs**
  2. **Tax shelters**
  3. **Tax-free money market funds**
  4. **Municipal bonds**
  5. **Tax-free bond mutual funds**
- **Use tax-deferred investment vehicles to promote capital growth. Divide retirement funds proportionately between:**
  Conservative investments **40%**
  Moderate investments **25%**
  Moderate-risk investments **25%**
  Risk investments **10%**

10
PREPARING FOR PARENTHOOD

One of the biggest changes in attitude between the last generation and this one is in the concept of parenthood. For the previous generation, it was the mother's job and duty to bear children and stay at home to raise them. It was the father's duty to earn enough money to provide a comfortable and secure home life for his family. There was no discussion of daycare, of maternity benefits, of how long a new mother should stay with her infant before going back to work, or of the professional drawbacks to having children at all.

Today's prospective parents have to consider all of the above and more when they plan their families. Preparations for parenthood are complicated: How long can we wait to have children? Whose job is going to go? How long a leave from work should be taken? What kind of childcare is most suitable? Such complications basically stem from the blurring of traditional roles that has occurred in the last generation as women deferred marriage and motherhood to start their careers. Suddenly, childrearing isn't a lifetime career. It has to be fit into an existing work schedule and it has to be shared by both parents.

The difficulties of balancing career and children, however, is offset by the economic advantages of the two-income family. Two-income families can afford children far better than one-income families. Even if one parent stays home during the early years of childrearing, he or she has had the time to plan for the hiatus and put money aside to cover living expenses. Statistics suggest that today's couples often wait eight or nine years until they have enough money set aside to be financially comfortable during the early childrearing years. Or, if they marry in their early or middle thirties, they may not wait long before becoming parents, but they've had many income-earning years behind them to segregate money so that they can afford parenthood without a struggle.

The issue for today's professional-couple-turned-parents is not how to stretch this week's grocery money with coupons as much as it is how to make the budget stretch to include daycare, babysitters, special programs for children, and entertainment for the parents as well. The question is, How are they going to become parents without completely losing the lifestyle they enjoy as a professional couple? And the answer is, Plan ahead.

Prospective parents should give careful consideration to their financial condition long before the baby is due home. They need to look for flexibility in their budget in case of unexpected costs. They also need to pad their short-term accounts to provide for a source of emergency financial funds during the pregnancy and the early years of parenthood. The following are three rules of thumb for financial security that all expecting parents should follow:

LEARNING TO LIVE ON ONE SALARY

Prospective parents should consider how they can get along on just the husband's salary if for some reason the pregnant wife needs to leave work early and/or has a protracted recuperation after childbirth. What kind of auxiliary funds would they need to augment one salary if the other one were absent for longer than expected?

One way to figure out how much additional income, if any, would be needed is to draw up a monthly expense budget reflecting any changes in spending that would accompany the wife's being at home. Some costs would go down, such as commuting and outside entertainment expenses. Others might go up, such as telephone, utility, home furnishings, and grocery bills. Then, subtract the wife's salary from the monthly budget and see if you have enough money to cover your proposed budget. If you don't, look over your assets for potential sources of income, such as the following:

Property Refinancing: Interest rates on mortgages can change dramatically in a short period of time. Is the rate on your mortgage competitive? If current interest rates are standing at 12 percent and the interest charged on your loan is 15 or 16 percent, consider refinancing your home. You might be able to bring down your monthly payments by $100 or more.

Of course you have to take into consideration the cost of getting the new mortgage. Closing costs can run up to several thousands of dollars. To make your new mortgage worth the extra expense, you have to stay in your present home for at least as long as it takes for the monthly savings to make up the amount of the closing costs. For example, if you paid $3,600 in closing costs on a new mortgage and your new payments saved you $200 a month, you'd need to stay in your home at least eighteen months to get back your closing costs.

Using Returns on Short-Term and Long-Term Investments: If you have been reinvesting the interest or dividends you receive on securities such as stocks or bonds, you should consider using that money as income if necessary. Go through your records and total up how much income you could expect to receive from your investments.

Restructuring Investment Portfolio: If most of your money is invested in long-term, growth-oriented products, you could restructure your portfolio for a limited time so that it would produce more income

SAVINGS YOU CAN EXPECT FROM REFINANCING:

	ORIGINAL MORTGAGE RATE	CURRENT MONTHLY PAYMENT	MONTHLY SAVINGS AT 13%	ANNUAL SAVINGS AT 13%
$60,000 mortgage	14.0%	$711	$47	$562
	14.5	735	71	850
	15.0	759	95	1,138
	15.5	783	119	1,426
	16.0	807	143	1,714
	16.5	832	167	2,009
	17.0	856	191	2,296
	17.5	880	216	2,592
$120,000	14.0%	$1,422	$94	$1,123
	14.5	1,470	142	1,699
	15.0	1,518	190	2,275
	15.5	1,566	238	2,851
	16.0	1,614	286	3,427
	16.5	1,663	335	4,018
	17.0	1,711	383	4,594
	17.5	1,760	432	5,184

Source: "How to Lighten a Heavy Mortgage," *Business Week*, 29 April 1985, originally from Mortgage Bankers Association of America.

by moving funds out of growth-oriented investments into income-producing securities, taxable or tax-free.

These ideas won't apply to everyone's financial situation. They do, however, provide an example of how to look at your monthly expenses and assets to find ways of lowering costs and increasing income in the event of an emergency. Look for expenses that can be lowered, put off, or cut altogether. Look at your investments for products that could throw off income if you needed it. If you need help determining what your options might be for lowering your monthly overhead and creating more income, ask your tax advisor or broker for assistance.

ADD UP THE COSTS OF EARLY PARENTHOOD

The next step in your financial preparations would be to add up the costs of caring for the baby during the months when the mother may not be earning her normal salary. Oftentimes, the initial setup costs of the nursery and layette are covered by gifts and hand-me-downs, but what about the day-to-day costs of a sitter or housekeeper, baby clothes, and pediatrician. Many new parents are unpleasantly surprised at how these costs mount up. Just a night out at the movies doubles in cost when you add in the babysitter. Talk to friends and relatives and find out what support services for parents cost in your area and what options are available to you. How much are diapers, food, formula, and other baby necessities likely to cost you a month? Once you've gathered some preliminary figures, sit down and work out an expense record for a month to find out if one income will cover your costs. If you find that your costs are too high, you can do some early planning to help bring them down or arrange to increase your income from investments.

After you have your contingency plan for the first few months following birth, you may want to look farther ahead to the first few years of childrearing. How much can parents expect to spend on their child in the first five years? An average cost is given below.

Housing	$ 8,393	(includes shelter, fuel, utilities, household operation, furnishings, and equipment)
Transportation	4,004	
Food at home	3,419	
Medical	1,405	
Clothing	930	
Food away from home	140	
All other	2,750	(includes personal care, recreation, and other miscellaneous expenses)
Total	$21,041	

Keep in mind when looking over these figures that they reflect costs for a typical midwestern family with a modest lifestyle where one partner stays at home as a caretaker. If you are accustomed to the very best, live in an expensive condominium, outfit your nursery with designer furniture, buy a closetful of clothes for the baby after every growth spurt, have full-time babysitting care for the first three years and then send your child to private nursery school, your costs for the first five years will be considerably greater. To get a figure closer to your reality, if you fall in this upwardly mobile group, add the cost of the services you intend to use, private nursery school, an additional clothing allowance based on a friend's experience, some percentage for inflation, as well as a more realistic cost for housing based on your current costs. This will give you a better estimate of what your expenses will be like for the first five years of parenthood.

To give you an idea of how vastly costs for childrearing vary depending on your location and lifestyle, consider the average expense of upwardly mobile new parents living in New York City during the first year of their child's life.

THE UPWARDLY MOBILE CHILD FIRST-YEAR COSTS:

Getting Started	$ 2,084.76
Making room*	14,193.80
Paying for child care	7,638.00
Necessities	1,987.31
Clothing	728.89
Equipment for outings	213.80
Safety measures	62.97
First books for baby	56.10
Milestones	711.89
	$27,677.52

* Presuming parents move to a larger apartment.

Source: "The High Cost of Baby-Booming," *New York Magazine*, 15 July 1985.

In other words, parents living in New York City can spend *more* in the first year of their child's life than the average midwestern parents spend in the first five years of their child's life.

BE PREPARED FOR EMERGENCIES

The third step in preparing for parenthood is to be prepared for emergencies. Plans for pregnancy and childbirth are often disrupted by unexpected occurrences. It would be wise to expand your emergency fund from three months' expenses to at least six months' expenses to cover surprises that can arise in the early stages of parenthood. Part of the extra emergency fund can come from a monthly savings plan, but part can also come from cashing in some of the investments you already have in place. If your growth stock mutual fund has already realized some capital gains over the last few years, you may want to take advantage of those long-term gains and sell some of your shares to add to your emergency fund. Conversely, if an investment isn't going the way you thought it would, you might want to cut your losses early and deposit the cash in a money market account that is liquid, interest-bearing, and available for daily use. Of course, short-term investments, such as certificates of deposit or Treasury bills, can also be cashed in at maturity and reinvested in a money market to help increase your liquid assets. If you're a self-directed investor, you'll know how best to appropriate the extra cash you need. However, if you depend on a broker for advice, ask him or her about the best way to fill up the emergency till.

These three preparatory steps not only make good economic sense, but good psychological sense as well. Early parenthood can be traumatic—especially for older parents with established lifestyles. You'll want to devote your energies to finding a routine that is comfortable for you and your new family, not to handling household budget crises.

PLANNING FOR THE FUTURE

Oftentimes, a hard transition for a professional-couple-turned-parents is the one from relative economic freedom to financial discipline. In the two-income household, quick trips to Bermuda, a splurge on theater tickets, or the upkeep of a high-performance car are easily affordable. However, once a child comes into the picture, spending has to become more planned. It's not that a weekend away, theater tickets, or a sports car are out of the picture; it's more a matter of taking care of priorities before putting out the money for discretionary spending. Such long-term financial planning often is not a habit with today's professional couples and requires some adjustment.

The most pressing issues for many parents today are housing and education. How long can we live in this luxury one-bedroom apartment with our two-year-old and the baby on the way? Should we buy a larger apartment or rent one? When is the right time to buy a vacation home out of the city? How can we prepare ourselves for the overwhelming burden of college tuition—not to mention private elementary schooling?

When considering these financial problems, parents should keep in mind that the solutions can also help them reduce their taxable income. For instance, it might be better to stay cramped up in a small apartment for an extra year if you'll then have the down payment on an apartment or first home that will provide you with deduction for tax payments and mortgage interest. Given today's high rents, buying an apartment or house might not cost you much more on a month-to-month basis than renting, and you'll be getting the tax advantages of ownership and equity.

Planning in advance makes the financing of a large purchase easier. As mentioned earlier, the down payment for a car or boat may be found in a collateral loan or a line of credit at your brokerage firm, both of which will save you interest over unsecured loans. If you have a low mortgage and interest rates aren't escalating, or are nearly finished paying off a first mortgage, refinancing a home is also a method of raising cash when you need it.

Your savings plans for private education and tuitions can also be arranged to lower your taxable income by transferring some money in the form of a nontaxable gift to your child's taxable estate. You can do this through a Uniform Gifts to Minors Account (UGMA).

The UGMA allows for a gift of up to $10,000 per year from anyone to a minor (usually under age eighteen) before a gift tax is incurred. The money is put into a custodial account opened under your child's social security number, but managed and controlled by the custodian of the account—usually the parents. Because the account is held in the child's name, however, the interest or dividends earned by the principal as well as any capital gain are taxed according to the child's tax bracket, which is usually low or nonexistent. This favorable tax situation may be altered, however, under the pending 1986 tax bill. Still, a child without substantial outside income will be in a benign status regarding taxes. A custodial UGMA can be set up with your bank, through a mutual fund, or through your brokerage house. Your decision on where to open the account will depend on how you intend to invest the contributions made over the years.

You are responsible for the management of the funds in a custodial account until control reverts to your child when he or she is an adult. You and/or your financial advisor can work out an investment plan that gives you a guaranteed income over the life of the trust (e.g., CDs or zero coupons), a chance for growth and income (e.g., blue-chip stocks), or a combination of both. You might also want to stagger the maturity dates of your investments in order to have the income in time for needs at different ages, such as private high school costs followed by college tuition.

A custodial account should be set up as soon as the child is born. You can put not only your own contributions into it, but also the cash gifts of friends and relatives. The $10,000 amount is the limit any one person can give to another each year. It is not the total amount that can be received. If your infant has every toy he or she can throw, pull, hit, stack, and roll, let your relatives know that what the baby needs for the next holiday is a contribution toward her future.

Of course, your contributions to the child's account will fluctuate greatly—especially in the early years. However, keep in mind that it's not important how much you put away for your child's future as much as that you put some amount away regularly. Keep in mind, too, that small investments with long periods of time to mature can make significant gains in value. For instance, a $1,000 zero coupon bond maturing in fifteen years currently costs as little as $180. That means that when your child is fifteen years old, your $180 investment will be worth $1,000—more than five times its original value.

Let's take a look at how a custodial account, set up at birth, might be used to fund a college education. In 1984, the average cost for one year of education at a private university (including tuition, room, and board) was $9,307. If you assume a modest tuition increase of 6 percent per year, the average cost of one year's education at a private university in the year 2000 will be $24,000. And if you are planning on sending your child to an Ivy League school, the cost could be half again as much. Thus, your minimum goal would have to be $100,000.

If you opened a UGMA for a newborn child in 1985, you could plan for a college tuition in the following way. You could make whatever contributions you could afford into a brokerage account that would be used to invest in zero coupon bonds maturing in each of four years—2003, 2004, 2005, and 2006. Zero coupons with a face value of $1,000 maturing in fifteen years cost about $180 per bond. You'd need to buy twenty-five bonds maturing in each of the above years to meet the average cost for a year at college. Therefore, you'd need to invest $4,500 in zero coupon bonds maturing in each of the years listed above to meet your basic expenses. You can buy your first bond when your child is three years old, so that gives you three years to build up the balance in your account to meet your goal. If you contributed $3,000 annually to your child's UGMA account from birth to six years of age, you'd have accumulated the amount of money you needed to buy the one hundred zero coupons necessary for the average cost of a college education. That's approximately $250 a month—less than many people pay for a car loan.

The main drawback to a UGMA for most parents is in the distribution of funds. The accumulated funds automatically go to the child—without restrictions on use—when he or she reaches the age of majority in your place of residence. Parents often have two concerns about this manner of distributing the accumulated funds: (1) the money won't go for its intended use and will instead be used unwisely, and (2) the parents won't have legal access to the funds after the child comes of age even if they suffer some financial emergency. These risks should be weighed against the benefits of taking the money out of your taxable estate when you consider a UGMA.

If you would rather maintain control of the tuition account after your child reaches adult age, consider tax-free zero coupons or tax-free municipal bonds purchased in your own name as vehicles for setting aside funds for education. These products can provide long-term earnings without a heavy tax burden.

Finally, some long-term goals may be met by investing wisely to maximize your earnings. For instance, you might pledge to yourself to add a set amount to your income mutual fund, child's custodial account, or money market at specified periods. Additional investments often can be made with as little as $200. By keeping your liquid assets in high-earning accounts, you are maximizing your return while you increase your original principal.

FOR PARENTS OF HANDICAPPED CHILDREN

The parents of a handicapped child are blessed with increasingly sophisticated methods of training to help their children grow into functional adults, and cursed with the tremendous cost of those services. Often, on top of the burden of childrearing itself comes the necessity of establishing some kind of fund that will support the child even after the parents are dead. Even if the handicapped child could earn a minimal living as well as have access to some government benefits, you'd still want to make sure that he or she could afford any medical help necessary throughout life.

Planning ahead while trying to avail your handicapped child of all opportunities for a special education can be difficult. But if you start a regular investment program at birth—however small the periodic contributions—you may be able to set up a substantial security fund for your child.

There are uncertainties in any investment, but when trying to protect a handicapped child, you want to be as secure as possible. First of all, you should have a will and in it name a guardian for your child. Something unforeseen could happen to you and/or your spouse and you should be assured that the monies you have set aside for your child are used as you had intended them to be.

Secondly, you should take out a higher than normally recommended life insurance policy on both yourself and your spouse, naming your child as the beneficiary. In this way, you provide some financial cushion if a disaster befalls you. Again, the designated guardian will know how to properly handle the insurance benefits.

Another long-term protective device is a lifetime trust for the child. Your own situation will dictate whether and under what conditions the child receives only the income from the trust, principal payments if necessary, or everything in the corpus of the trust. It is extremely important that the intention of the trust is spelled out in detail so that the money you leave to protect your disabled child is not used inappropriately, such as to pay debts or to replace government benefits. These details should be worked out with a tax and estate lawyer. Again, you will want to cover as many contingencies as possible.

By now, you can see that the key to successful money management for parents is long-range planning that takes into account as many unexpected variables as possible. The earlier you start planning for the future, the more headway you'll have made if unforeseen financial setbacks temporarily interrupt your progress toward a final goal. Parents need flexibility in their budgets. They need to be able to take money from one targeted area and apply it to a more immediate need, such as unexpected medical or educational expenses.

Some parents put off planning for tomorrow thinking that their incomes will be greater in the future and make saving easier and more efficient. Sometimes discretionary income does increase greatly later in life, but as often as not, expenses increase just as quickly, making targeted goals as difficult to reach as they were during lean years. It's best to establish a habit of funneling money toward your known future financial obligations as early as possible to make sure that you have the money you need. If you reach your goal before you need the money, then you can be more liberal in your own spending without worry.

Financial goals for parents:
- **Map out alternate means of support during pregnancy or the postpartum period when partner's income is uncertain.**
- **Be financially prepared for emergencies.**
- **Estimate the cost of childrearing in your location.**
- **Prepare for your child's future by opening a custodial account at birth.**

11
FOR SINGLE PARENTS

The single parent has evolved from the pariah of our parents' generation to the subject of prime-time sitcoms in our generation. Whether divorced, single by choice, or widowed, the financial concerns of single parents are less different from their married counterparts than they are magnified. Instead of two people trying to find the time and money to raise their children well, one person is faced with the complete task. One person has to pay the doctor bills, the babysitter, and the cost of new tennis shoes, designer jeans, and the bike that is a must. To the single parent, the cost of raising a child can seem overwhelming; however, careful financial planning can ease the burden, just as it does for married parents.

The first thing that any single parent should do is create a new Personal Financial Profile detailing his or her expenses, assets, income from other sources (e.g., child support, alimony, maintenance), debts, and long-term financial commitments. The purpose is twofold: first, it gives the single parent economic boundaries so that he or she won't feel adrift financially, and second, it sets a point of departure for future financial planning. Developing a financial plan is necessary for all single parents, but the goal of the exercise will vary depending on whether divorce, death, or choice was behind the change in lifestyle.

SINGLE PARENTHOOD BY CHOICE

For the single man or woman who decides to become a parent, the changes in spending habits will take some getting used to. The single individual's basic living expenses may be moderate, including rent or mortgage payments on a studio apartment, utilities, car loan, and insurance payments. However, travel, entertainment, and clothing expenses probably take up a considerable amount of discretionary income.

Becoming a parent changes that spending picture. Live-in or live-out babysitters and housekeepers cost several hundred dollars a month. Medical bills, clothing, preschool tuition, and other educational expenses as well as an increase in rent or mortgage for a residence that accommodates your new family member all can cut drastically into the money available for theater subscriptions, summer houses, long weekends in the Caribbean, seasonal wardrobes, and fine dining.

If you're a prospective single parent, you need to examine carefully the extent to which parenthood would change your lifestyle before making the commitment to this new role. Make sure that the financial burdens will not outweigh the desire for a child in a few months.

You can forecast the change in your lifestyle by creating a Personal Financial Review that reflects the estimated cost of raising a child. As would any expecting parent, you should ask other new parents in your neighborhood about the costs of childcare, proper medical care, clothes, nursery school, formula, diapers, bottles, and so on. Add in a reasonable rent for a larger apartment, if you intend to move, and then tally up your new monthly financial obligation:

Rent or mortgage _____
(include maintenance or tax payments)

Utilities _____

Food _____
(include formula or other baby food costs)

Diapers _____
(or diaper service)

Childcare _____
(include fees for preschool activities and classes)

Life insurance _____

House insurance _____

Medical insurance _____

Pediatrician _____

Clothing _____
(for you and the baby)

Miscellaneous _____
(dry cleaning, cosmetics, haircuts, toys, books, etc.)

Once you've determined your monthly expenses, compare them to your current spending habits. Are your newly calculated basic monthly expenses greater? Will you be spending more money for everyday living costs so that less will be available for recreation?

Your proposed budget will help you understand what becoming a parent is going to mean to you financially and how it will affect your current spending habits. Will the budget restraints be too confining? Or will they become part of a welcome change in your lifestyle?

SUDDENLY SINGLE

In the case of a sudden death or divorce, there often isn't a choice about whether or not to assume the full financial obligations of parenthood. They are thrust upon the partner taking responsibility for the children. Budgeting and planning won't present a problem for the single parent accustomed to handling household finances. However, widowed and divorced parents unfamiliar with money management may develop haphazard spending habits that erode the family's financial security. They may resort to expensive credit lines, borrowing against securities in a brokerage account, or selling investments prematurely to pay everyday expenses. Then when the proceeds from the assets are needed for college tuition or the purchase of a house, the funds aren't available.

This lack of foresight in spending isn't necessarily a sign of irresponsibility on the part of the newly single parent. It may instead be a reflection of ignorance and panic. Suddenly you're alone and the bills are sitting in an ominous stack on your desk. A widow or recently divorced parent may worry about touching emergency funds and feel that it's safer to use a credit line. In fact, the opposite is true. This is the time to tap your emergency funds while you leave the rest of your financial estate intact until you devise a strategy that will meet your daily needs and your future obligations. Your "freedom money" can give you breathing room to recuperate emotionally and plan for the future.

For the financially naïve, an important step toward planning future security is to consult with an expert about how to structure your finances. Some banks offer financial planning services, and you can always turn to a broker for advice. Advice from a professional money manager will help you use your income and existing assets to meet your future obligations as well as to provide for your daily living expenses.

The overall financial concerns of divorced and widowed parents are similar, but the resources they have to work with often are quite different.

FOR DIVORCED PARENTS

For the divorced parent, the main problem is matching up cash income and outflow. The parent with custody of the child has to arrange the household budget around child support, tuition, and/or maintenance payments. The parent paying for child support, tuition, and/or maintenance has to set up a financial plan that takes those regular payments into account. Both divorced partners have to work out a plan whereby their budget is controlled to allow for tax-advantaged and retirement investments. By approaching all of these financial goals one at a time, creating a money management strategy doesn't seem so daunting. The following three guidelines can help you get started:

Revise your investment strategy.

A divorced parent facing an increase in living expenses needs to scrutinize his or her current investments to determine if the goal of the assets is still viable. For instance, if your money was placed largely in growth stocks for capital gain rather than income-producing securities, you may want to reconsider those investments if cash flow is a problem. Perhaps some of the holdings should be exchanged for income-producing stocks to help you meet immediate financial obligations. Income stock or bond purchases would be a far better answer to cash flow problems than credit lines or investment liquidation. With these income-producing products, you have the chance to increase your worth at the same time that you are deriving income from the investment.

Another example of an investment that may need to be rethought is property. If a house is part of your settlement, consider it in the light of its investment value. Do you need the space? Would you be better off selling the house and buying a smaller residence or a condominium for which the carrying charges would be lower? If your house has appreciated a great deal, you may realize a profit that is greater than the cost of buying your new, smaller home. The extra funds can go toward future obligations, such as college tuition or your own retirement.

These are two examples of how restructuring investments can lead to greater income. However, there are as many investment strategies as there are divorced parents, and each single parent will have to map out a plan that works best for the financial conditions circumscribing his or her life.

After you've worked out an appropriate investment strategy, you'll have a better idea of how much income you can expect to receive from your assets on a regular basis. Add this figure to your known income as well as any child support or alimony you'll be receiving and go on to define your financial needs.

Map out your financial needs and goals.

This is an essential part of building a sound financial base for any single parent. You need to sit down and juggle figures to come up with a workable budget. First, put down your ideal expense budget and compare it with your income. You might find that you have enough money to lead the lifestyle of your preference. However, if your expenses exceed your income, or if they leave no room for contributions toward future needs, you'll have to scale back some of your costs. Maybe you can share a babysitter or take your child to a recommended in-home daycare center rather than incur the higher expense of hiring a private babysitter. Maybe you'll have to trade your entertainment subscriptions for individual performance ticket purchases when you can afford them. Or perhaps you'll decide that a rental in the suburbs would just make more sense at this time rather than trying to cope with the exorbitant cost of city life.

You're the only person who knows what is essential in your life and what can be given up without great discomfort, so you're the best person to decide what will stay and what will go. Try to come up with a few ways for cutting your proposed budget so that you have several options to choose from.

Prepare for the future.

The prospect of getting by from paycheck to paycheck as a single parent seems difficult enough without adding the burden of salting money aside for emergencies or future obligations. Besides, how much could you put away? Twenty-five, fifty dollars a month? That's not going to amount to much, especially if you measure it against the sums you were putting away before the divorce.

This is a common misconception made by single—or married—parents who can make only small annual contributions to education and retirement funds. In fact, these sums are important. Keep in mind that small sums of money put aside for many years can gain considerably in value. For instance, a $1,000 face amount zero coupon bond paying a little over 10 percent interest that matures in fifteen years costs only $180 to buy today. Invested wisely today, $500 could be worth $2,500 when your child goes to school.

But the amount of money you put away and what happens to it is only part of the reason for making regular contributions toward future financial goals. The *habit* of regular contributions is important by itself, regardless of the amount put aside. It's a habit you want to establish now, even though money is tight, so that it's ingrained by the time the economic crisis is over and you're earning enough money to commit larger sums toward future obligations. Single parents who are waiting till money loosens up a bit before they start planning for tomorrow often find that the opportunity never arises.

The divorced parent who takes these three steps will be able to eliminate one of the most pressing concerns of single parenthood: present and future financial security.

FOR SURVIVING PARENTS

Unlike divorced parents, surviving parents don't have a problem of cash flow as much as they do a problem of investment and planning for the future. Most survivors will come into a lump sum of money and have to invest that inheritance to provide for present family needs as well as future expenses.

What concerns are greatest for surviving parents? The same ones that any single parent has: childcare, housing, and educational costs. This age group feels especially vulnerable about future expenses. They usually haven't reached their peak earning years and haven't had a chance to put a great deal of money aside for future costs. Suddenly, perhaps, the economic partner is lost. How is the surviving parent going to realize the financial future planned before the death?

Once again, a structured approach for reorganizing financial affairs will ease the transition from married to single parent. The following financial protocol is particularly helpful for a widowed parent who may find it hard to address everyday concerns soon after the emotional shock of losing a partner.

Inaction is the best action.

For the bereaved parent, the first step toward a secure future is inaction. The emotional shock of a spouse's death often leaves one unable to make sound judgments on household and financial matters. Too much attention may be paid to well-meaning or not-so-well-meaning advisors and friends. A widow may simply want to get rid of these financial problems and dump all of the money into one investment or another on the advice of a friend. Too often, when the surviving parent is finally ready and capable of turning attention to family finances, the net worth of the inheritance is halved or worse.

If possible, the surviving parent should leave the estate as it stands for six months or so until the initial emotional shock has worn off. However, if the widowed parent is forced to take some action with a large sum of money, the best investment would be in the safest short-term investment available, such as a Treasury bill or a certificate of deposit. The money will earn interest and remain secure until the surviving parent can effectively plan for the future.

Protect the new family.

If the surviving parent is not holding life insurance, he or she should make sure that a policy is drawn up to protect the surviving child or children. Also, a new will is necessary to define how assets should be used in the event of the second parent's death, as well as to establish a guardian for the children if none was chosen before.

Find out where you stand.

The widowed parent's personal financial review will be the cornerstone of his or her investment strategy. It will provide a broad view of assets as well as a detailed account of current expenses that need to be covered by those assets. The widowed parent needs to draw up a new monthly budget that will include any new costs of single parenthood, for example, daycare, live-in housekeeper, or life insurance. The listing will not only serve as a guide for financial planning, but will also help the widowed partner grasp the new responsibilities of single parenthood.

Plan for today and tomorrow.

Once the widowed parent feels emotionally prepared to assume the responsibilities of household financier, he or she should seek out professional guidance in managing the estate left by the deceased partner. Even if the single parent has handled the family's investments and budgets in the past and feels competent to direct the investment of the inheritance, he or she should at least get an outside opinion on the proposed management of the estate to make sure that every financial need and tax situation is addressed as well as possible.

The two concerns of a surviving parent are how to pay for day-to-day expenses, and how to plan a secure future for both the parent and the child using and maintaining the inheritance.

Day-to-day expenses: The goal of the investment program will be to use as little of the actual inheritance as possible to pay for living expenses. To the greatest extent possible, basic necessities will be paid for by income earned on investments made with the inheritance. In this way, the estate will provide for the family at the same time that value will be kept intact or even increased.

Financing the Future: A widowed parent can plan for the future using the same tools as any other parent. A Uniform Gifts to Minors Account offers the parent a depository for investments that will be taxed at the child's low income bracket. However, if the single parent is concerned about how well the child will handle funds in early adulthood, tax-free municipal bonds and tax-free zero coupons held in the parent's name can also be used to build a financial future without increasing taxable income. By investing in bonds with staggered maturities, a widowed parent can secure a child's financial future through college and on into early adulthood.

The same principle used to finance a child's future can be used to finance the surviving parent's future. Long-term investments that can provide a steady income in later years are attractive because the initial investment often is small next to the eventual value of the security. However, investments need not be limited to such conservative instruments as municipal bonds and zero coupons. A widowed parent at this stage of life who can afford to take a little risk in the hope of reaping a greater gain might look at quality growth stocks, discount bonds, or a precious metals mutual fund. Also, for the surviving parent who is in a high tax bracket, a tax-advantaged limited partnership might be a good investment that will provide long-term capital gains and an immediate tax deduction.

Becoming a single parent, whether by choice or by unforeseen life changes, is a difficult transition even in the best circumstances. A great many of the concerns of single parents revolve around finances: How will I prepare myself for retirement and afford college tuition at the same time? What will happen to my family if I'm unable to work? How can I construct a financial bulwark for my children that will protect them in the event of my death? The steps given previously provide a money management framework for single parents that will help them create a financial foundation designed to answer these critical questions.

Single Parents:
1. **Estimate cost of parenthood.**
2. **Budget for a new lifestyle.**
3. **Plan for the future.**

Divorced Parents:
1. **Match income with cash flow.**
2. **Make a habit of investing for the future.**
3. **Target investment strategy to meet needs of new lifestyle.**

Surviving Parents:
1. **Take time to recover emotionally.**
2. **Get assistance or second opinion on estate planning.**
3. **Pay as much of day-to-day budget as possible with income thrown off from existing investments.**

12
YOUR INSURANCE NEEDS

The insurance needs of this age group will vary greatly from the early part of this stage to the later part. For twenty-five-year-olds who are single and childless, insurance is a simple affair meant to cover losses of personal effects as a result of theft or fire. For the thirty-nine-year-old with two children, a house, and a collection of valuable personal effects, however, insurance needs are more complicated.

HOUSEHOLD INSURANCE

Let's first take a look at property insurance that anyone who lives on his or her own should have. This insurance often is inexpensive compared to the peace of mind it provides in the case of a burglary or fire. Even for the young adult starting out, it pays to think about what it would cost to replace the television, cassette player, stereo, computer, and VCR if they were taken. Or, in the case of a fire, could you afford to start over buying a bed, couch, armoire, and dining table as well as the items mentioned above? Rather than take the chance of having to cover these expenses yourself, you should talk to an insurance agent—either your parents' agent or one recommended by a colleague or friend. Find out what kind of coverage is recommended in your area and how much it will cost. Also find out if any security precautions—pick-resistant locks, window bars—reduce the cost of your insurance.

Once you've gotten your policy, don't make the mistake of putting it in the back of your file and forgetting about it. As we mentioned earlier, members of this age group work to acquire the accouterments of the lifestyle they want to have. One year you may buy a stereo to replace your old record player. The next year you put money aside for a fur coat or new car. Every time you make major purchases such as these, you need to update your insurance coverage. It's wise to take out your policy periodically—say, when you do your tax review at the end of the year—and make sure that you're covered for new acquisitions.

Another time you need to reassess your insurance is when you bring in a new roommate. Both of you will have to sit down and draw up a list of belongings that are owned separately and jointly. If you had insurance before your roommate moved in, you'll want the policy adjusted to include his or her belongings. The premium can be split according to the amount of insurance needed by each roommate. For instance, let's say that basic fire insurance costs $100 a year. You split that cost down the middle. But your roommate has a collection of fine antique tea cups and several costly pieces of furniture. Her insurance alone comes to another $75 while yours is $50 for your new stereo and second-hand furnishings. For this part of the premium, each roommate can cover the cost of insuring his or her belongings.

HEALTH AND DISABILITY INSURANCE

Most of us who work for large companies take health and disability insurance for granted. But for employees of small companies or for self-employed workers, these insurance needs can pose a significant financial burden. Individual coverage from Blue Cross/Blue Shield or any other major medical carrier can cost $1,000 and over. Because of the high price of health insurance, uncovered individuals in this group may shrug off the need for it. After all, they're young, healthy, never broke a bone in their lives. However, health insurance is a necessity given the exorbitant costs of hospitalization. A bed alone in a private hospital can cost upwards of $250 for one night. That's not including any services, meals, medical attention, or drugs. A stay in the hospital without coverage can be devastating.

Though health insurance is an expensive necessity, you may be able to lessen the cost by applying for your coverage through a professional society that obtains group rates for members who work independently.

Disability insurance is not as critical as health insurance. However, individuals with long-term or chronic illnesses that may limit their earning capacity should consider making this investment. The insurance provides the beneficiary with a predetermined percent of his or her regular income for a specified period of time should he or she become incapacitated. The length of benefits as well as the percentage of salary varies from policy to policy.

LIFE INSURANCE OPTIONS

Life insurance doesn't become an issue for most people in this stage of life until they decide to have children. Usually, the expectant parents will wait until the child is born to purchase their insurance. It might be wise, though, to consider a partial purchase of life insurance during the pregnancy so that the surviving expectant or new parent will have some financial security in case of an unexpected calamity. What kind and how much insurance you purchase will depend on many factors in your personal life: income, overhead, place of residence, number of children, and so on. You'll have to depend on your insurance agent to help you determine how much insurance will be adequate for your needs. As is the case with any financial advisor, it's important to find an insurance agent in whom you can have confidence to make these decisions. A reference from a friend, your broker, or your lawyer is your best method of finding a competent insurance agent.

Your agent will help you match your needs with one or a combination of the following types of life insurance:

Term Insurance: These policies are sold for short periods of time such as one, five, or ten years. Premiums are set according to your age when you purchase the policy and will change every time you buy a new term policy. The advantage of these policies is that you make a financial commitment only for short periods rather than for a lifetime, and premiums are often less expensive than those for whole life policies. Your policy provides you with death benefits for the beneficiary and nothing else.

The limited benefits provided by term insurance, however, can also be one of its disadvantages. Unlike other forms of life insurance, your policy doesn't gain *cash surrender value*. Cash surrender value, or cash value, is derived from the cash reserve that builds up as premiums are paid on a life policy that never expires. The cash reserve from the premiums is invested by the insurance company to earn interest income that is credited to your account. The interest income provides the savings feature of the straight life policy. Over the years, the interest income builds up the cash value of your policy that you can borrow against (usually at lower interest than banks or brokerage loans) or take out as income. Term insurance, which has a limited premium payment period, doesn't build up a cash reserve or offer the savings feature that provides a cash surrender value.

Whole Life: Whole life insurance is a much more diversified investment than term insurance. You're buying the policy for the death benefit, but you're receiving several other financial benefits as well. Whole life policies include a provision for the accumulation of cash value over the life of the loan as well as for investment income on the cash value of the policy. The cash value and accumulated investment income can be used as collateral to borrow against, or, if you terminate the policy, to recoup part of your premium costs.

Traditional whole life policies have a set benefit and premium determined at the time of purchase. Neither the benefit nor the premium would change unless you alter the policy.

The kind of investment income you receive on the cash value of your insurance will depend on the type of policy and insurance carrier. Traditional whole life insurance has a lower rate of return than other investment opportunities. Therefore, in order to compete with other financial institutions for investor dollars, insurance carriers recently increased the potential rates of return on the cash value of insurance policies by creating several new kinds of policies. Today's whole life insurance options include the following:

Traditional whole life policies offer a set benefit and premium that remains the same for the life of the policy. The return you receive on your cash value will be either a predetermined interest if your carrier is a "stock life insurance company," or dividends if your carrier is a mutual life insurance company that treats its policy owners as shareholders. In the latter case, the dividends can be used to increase the cash value or the death benefit of the policy. If you buy a policy from a mutual life insurance company, you should take a look at the company's performance for the last few years to see what your expected rate of return in the form of dividends will be.

Universal life policies offer a combination of the benefits of term and whole life policies. You buy insurance for a predetermined number of years, but instead of the whole premium going only to finance the death benefit, part of it pays for a side investment that allows the policy to accumulate cash value like a whole life policy. The premium payments of universal life policies are also flexible, meaning that you can postpone payments if you need cash for other purposes, then adjust future premiums to cover the payments you missed.

You'll pay for the privileges that come with a universal life policy. In general the cost of these policies is higher than for more traditional policies. Make sure that the flexibility you gain is not outweighed by the extra cost you incur when you consider this kind of insurance.

Single-premium life insurance calls for a one-time premium payment that is usually $5,000 or over. The emphasis in this kind of insurance is less on the insurance coverage than on the cash value of the policy. The return you get for your investment is greater than in other kinds of policies, but the insurance coverage may be less. Thus, investors find a good value here, but those seeking the most insurance coverage for the lowest cost should look elsewhere.

Variable life insurance offers a combination of whole life and term insurance as does universal life insurance; part of your premium goes toward a term insurance policy, and part goes to an investment program that helps you accumulate cash value. However, the difference between these two kinds of insurance is the insured's control over his or her investments in variable life policies. The investment premiums will be used to buy securities—such as money market products, stocks, or bonds—but you can choose the instruments best suited to your needs. One person may prefer to put the whole cash value in blue-chip stocks while another may want a combination of a money market fund and a top-quality bond. Because of this unique investment aspect, variable life insurance policies are sold by registered securities dealers rather than through a mutual or stock life insurance company.

Another benefit of variable life policies is the ability of the insured to change his or her investment strategy to keep earnings high. When interest rates are lower, for instance, a policy holder may move money out of money market instruments and into other high-growth investments instead.

As we will discuss in later chapters, your insurance needs will fluctuate as your lifestyle changes. Thus, the life insurance that seems right for your situation today may be inadequate or superfluous in a few years. Don't forget to look over your insurance policies whenever you make a change in your lifestyle, such as moving, marrying, having children, divorcing, or retiring. And even if your life remains stable, it's a good idea to check the value of your insurance each year as you pay your annual premiums to make sure that your coverage is adequate.

Insuring Adequate Coverage:
- **Review your insurance needs annually with your broker.**
- **Increase coverage when necessary to protect new acquisitions.**
- **Combine various types of life insurance policies to get the most coverage for your money.**

13
RETIREMENT CONSIDERATIONS

Retirement is not something in the forefront of most young adults' minds. In this age group, you're either just starting out or else just getting into the thick of housing or family expenses. Either way, you're probably stretched to the limit financially. The last thing you're even thinking about is putting aside money for retirement. After all, you've barely started to work.

In this generation, as opposed to our parents', the illusion of youth stays with us long into our mature years. We are part of the baby boom, the youth culture. We still listen to rock and roll and lead the way in fashion and spending. But the fact is that the youth culture of the 1960s and 1970s is moving into middle age and acquiring all the trappings of that stage of life—homes, children, property taxes, and station wagons (albeit foreign ones). And another reality is that when this great population bulge moves on to retirement, there's not going to be a great pool of young workers to shore up the social security system. Chances are that some benefits will be available, but they alone aren't going to support the lifestyle to which baby boomers are accustomed.

In the last generation, retirement funds were the nest egg that you built up in a savings account over the years. You figured that your house would be paid off, your children would be on their own, and you would be staying put after the trip abroad that you'd planned for years. You were looking forward to a quiet time when your social security and the interest from your nest egg could keep you comfortably if you were careful. And if you became infirm, your children would take care of you.

For the most part, that picture of retirement is obsolete. For one thing, life expectancies are longer. Early years of retirement often occur when retirees are still feeling strong and capable. Many people sell their homes and move to retirement complexes in the Sunbelt. Other people embark on second or third careers. The money you set aside has to support a secure yet active lifestyle often for twenty rather than ten years. And at the same time, it has to be able to cover the enormous expense of long-term medical and nursing care, not only for you, but quite possibly for your ailing, elderly parents as well. You might expect to pay for *your* parents, but you don't believe that your own children—flung far and wide in various careers—will come to your aid in old age.

The money to support an enjoyable long retirement isn't going to come just from social security and the company retirement plan. You're going to need investments that will provide income throughout your later years. Yet where are you going to get the money to put away after taxes, mortgage payments, school tuitions, and medical bills? The answer is that you're going to handle your retirement in the same manner that you would handle your children's college tuitions. You're going to start on a program very early, putting away modest amounts of money on a regular basis, and building up your retirement funds slowly through contributions and reinvestment of interest or dividends. And the government, recognizing your overburdened budget and your need for future security, is going to help you through their tax-advantaged retirement programs: IRAs and Keoghs.

The money in these accounts cannot be withdrawn without penalty until you are 59.5 years of age, a good incentive to leave the money untouched to multiply into a handsome retirement income.

IRAs

As was mentioned earlier, you can put any amount up to $2,000 per year into an IRA, although annual contributions are not mandatory. The contribution is tax-deductible, and the interest or dividends earned in your IRA is tax-deferred until you begin to draw from the account.

The question that always comes up when the restrictions on IRA withdrawals are explained is, What if you need the money before you're 59.5? You can get at the money if you really need to. You'll have to pay taxes plus a 10 percent penalty on what you withdraw, but even with those expenses, you might come out ahead. Remember that not only your contribution is tax-deductible, but all of the earnings reinvested into the account are tax-deferred until the money is withdrawn. Thus, you're going to keep more of an annual 10 percent earned on your IRA fund tax-free than you would of 10 percent earned on a taxable investment, and your investment is going to grow more rapidly. Because of this accelerated growth, you can withdraw money from your IRA in an emergency earlier than at age 59.5 without necessarily losing money. For instance, if you were to invest $2,000 per year in both an IRA and a taxable investment earning 10 percent interest a year, you'd come to a break-even point in four and a half years when, even considering the penalty for early withdrawal, your IRA investment would have earned the same amount of interest as the taxable investment.

Knowing that your money will be available in an emergency should remove the major obstacle in the way of taking full advantage of the benefits of an IRA by making regular contributions from as early an age as possible. The longer your money remains in your IRA, the longer it can compound tax-deferred in high-earning, long-term investments.

Timing of contributions is also important. You can wait until April 15 of the following tax year to make your contribution, but stalling is not to your advantage because your money then has less time to earn tax-deferred income. Look at what happens to an annual $2,000 contribution over a ten-, twenty-, and thirty-year period when the contribution is made on January 1, June 1, December 31, and the following April 15. (The figures below assume a 10 percent interest rate for the duration of the investment.)

PERIOD	JAN. 1	JUNE 1	DEC. 31	FOLLOWING APRIL 15
10 years	$ 35,062	$ 33,467	$ 31,874	$ 29,195
20 years	126,005	120,274	114,550	109,989
30 years	361,886	345,429	328,988	319,548

Source: Shearson Lehman Bros.

As you can see, in just ten years, you can earn an extra $5,867 by making your annual contribution at the beginning of the tax year instead of waiting until the following April 15. In thirty years, the early contribution can earn you an extra $42,338. The reason for this greater gain obviously is because your money has fifteen months longer to work for you every tax year when you make your contribution in January.

The funds in your IRA can be distributed among a variety of investments offered by up to three different custodian institutions (financial concerns functioning as custodian of your IRA account). In other words, one IRA could have investment in CDs bought from a bank, stocks purchased through a broker, and shares in a mutual fund. Given this flexibility, you can gain particularly high interest one year in a CD, and buy good zero coupon value bonds the next. Another year you may select a level 3 or even level 4 stock.

When choosing your IRA investments, you should look back over your investment quiz and the investment pyramid (see chapter 7). Part of your funds can be used for moderate investments while others can go into conservative and very conservative products. High-risk investments, however, are not advised because the legal cap on annual contributions makes it impossible to make up for your losses in many instances. For instance, if you contribute $2,000 one year and lose $500 of it in a high-risk investment, you can't put in another $500 that year to make up the loss. Good choices for an IRA include CDs, zero coupon bonds, income or high-yield mutual funds, and even income-oriented limited partnerships such as real estate programs.

KEOGH PLANS

If you're self-employed or earn income outside of your salaried job, you're also eligible to contribute to another tax-deductible retirement fund—the Keogh plan. Contributions to Keoghs or the now expanded deferred contribution plans currently can run up to $30,000 annually. Keogh contributions can be made on top of IRA contributions, thereby further reducing your taxable income.

Rules for withdrawal from Keoghs are similar to those for IRAs. You can't start to withdraw before the age of 59.5 without paying a penalty. However, the same "break-even" point also exists where the earnings on your investments—even after the premature withdrawal penalty—equal those on a taxed investment.

Investment advice for these accounts is similar to that for IRAs, although you have a wider choice of investments because of the larger sums you are allowed to set aside each year. Preservation of capital with a high compounding of interest or dividends is your aim.

It's often hard to understand what your retirement contribution will mean to you in thirty years when you need it right now to pay for the down payment on a new car. On the other hand, when you consider that a $2,000 IRA contribution earning 10 percent tax-deferred will double in seven years, you're likely to be persuaded to put that money into a retirement fund. To give you a better idea of how your early retirement can work for you, let's look at a hypothetical IRA account into which $2,000 has been contributed annually for twenty-five years and which has been earning a 10 percent return on those funds:

Total contributions would amount to $50,000. Interest earned on that sum would total $166,364, so the account balance would be $216,364. If you started to withdraw the money when you were sixty-five, you could have a monthly income of $2808 until you were seventy-five, or $2027 until you were eighty-five.

You can see in that example how your money can multiply again and again in these retirement plans with very little effort on your part. That may be incentive enough to keep your contributions regular, but if you need an added reason, remember that retirement accounts are one of the best tax-advantaged investments you can make. They not only give you money for the future, they also put more money in your pocket today by reducing your taxable income.

Part III

AN EYE ON THE FUTURE: INVESTMENT STRATEGIES FOR AGES 45-60

14
GOALS FOR THE MIDDLE YEARS

Remember those birthday cards you got your dad when he turned forty-five? There was always some balding, paunchy fellow on the front looking dolefully at himself in the mirror. The card made some joke about how it wasn't so bad getting old. That was last generation's middle years; you were past your prime when you entered your forties. You were starting to wind down.

Today it almost seems as if the reverse is true. The middle years are more and more thought of as the best. They are the years when the early struggles are over. You're doing the hiring and firing. You've got a standing reservation at your favorite three-star restaurant. Your kids, if not independent, are certainly out of diapers and in school. The monthly payments on your house and car that seemed overwhelming are easy to make now. You've got the time and money to go to a health club regularly, and you can afford to buy clothing that will show off your good condition. In short, these are the years when you are in command.

Far from being a time to wind down toward retirement, the middle years in this generation can be the stage of life with the greatest number of responsibilities. Because many baby boomers put off marriage until their late twenties or early thirties, they're likely to be immersed in parental duties at a time when our parents were sending the last of their children off to college. On the other hand, parenting isn't the struggle it was for our parents. Today's older parents have had more income-producing years to accumulate the funds needed to support children and to afford childcare services. So, while their primary parenting years could even last up until or beyond early retirement, the chore will be eased by greater financial resources.

Because of the high divorce rate in this generation, the middle years are also becoming a time of new beginnings for divorced people who remarry. Men—and women more and more—are starting second families during this stage of life. Even though these born-again parents are in their peak earning years, coping with the triple burden of providing for their new families, fulfilling their obligations to their first families *and* preparing for retirement requires skillful money management.

SPECTER OF THE FUTURE

Though you may be exhilarated by the heady atmosphere of success and achievement during these years, you may also be confronted by a variety of occurrences in your personal lives that underscore the need to prepare for the future. A parent may begin to require more and longer-term medical care. College education may seem a more immediate concern when children enter high school and start talking about their choice of schools. Toward the end of this stage colleagues at work begin to retire, allowing you not only to climb up to the top rungs on the corporate ladder, but to move into the last stages of your career as well.

Fortunately, you are at a point where you've acquired most of the services, products, or real estate that you need to live comfortably. By now, your income should exceed the cost of keeping up your lifestyle so that you have considerable money left over to invest for the future.

The best way to meet your changing needs as you move from early to middle adulthood is to review and alter the financial strategy you formulated earlier using the Five Steps of money management.

THE FIVE STEPS TO MANAGING YOUR MONEY

STEP 1: MAXIMIZE YOUR LIQUIDITY.

Cash flow is not a problem now. You've got your liquid assets in a money market fund, a brokerage account, or some other higher-interest-bearing account that offers check-writing privileges. Your day-to-day budget is fairly constant. Now is the time to look at some of your past investments to see if they can be used as sources of cash, or if they should be updated to decrease your living expenses or overall outlay of cash.

One investment that almost surely is worth more today is a house or apartment bought ten or fifteen years ago. A house that has increased in value is a good source of cash for expenses such as renovations or adding a room or basement. Also, in the event that the tuition costs you face are greater than the education funds you set aside, you might consider refinancing your home to meet those expenses. Keep in mind that a second mortgage needn't extend the traditional thirty years. Many banks offer fifteen-year mortgages at reduced interest rates. Often for as little as an extra $100 per month in mortgage payments, you'll be able to save fifteen years worth of interest charges—50 percent of the interest charged on a traditional thirty-year mortgage.

Even if you aren't looking for an available source of cash, you should review your mortgage commitment anyway every five years or so. Are the terms of your personal agreement in line with those that you could get today? For instance, if you were one of the first home buyers to take on a variable rate mortgage, you might be locked into a loan agreement that has no caps on the variation in the interest from year to year or over the life of the loan. Today most variable rate mortgages offer caps on annual change in interest rate (commonly 1 to 2 percent every year) and an overall cap on the interest rate variation over the life of the loan (commonly five to six percentage points above or below the initial interest charged). These caps offer you a stability in your financial planning that your present mortgage doesn't offer. Would it make sense to pay your closing costs anew to have the security of a cap on your variable mortgage interest rate?

You should also consider whether or not a lower interest rate mortgage would reduce your mortgage payments enough to justify taking on closing costs of a few thousand dollars. If you're planning to stay in your home for the time it would take for the difference between your current mortgage payment and your new mortgage payment to pay off the closing fees, then it makes sense to refinance. However, chasing lower interest rates every year doesn't make sense because it will cost you more in closing fees than it will save you in lower mortgage payments.

In some rare instances, you might find it worthwhile to prepay an outstanding balance as it is virtually all principal in the last years and, therefore, not tax-deductible. (Mortgage payments are split up into interest and principal. In the early years, your payments are nearly all interest, which is tax deductible. Out of a $630 payment, for instance, maybe only $200 is principal. The rest is deductible interest. This ratio of principal to interest reverses itself, however, in the last years of a mortgage so that the majority of the payment is nondeductible principal.)

You should also adjust the kind of money market account you have to fit your current needs. Most offer taxable returns on your money, but some offer tax-exempt returns. Are you in a bracket now where the tax-exempt money market fund will significantly increase the return on your liquid assets?

STEP 2: CONSOLIDATE ASSETS.

When you were just starting out, you gathered up all the odds and ends of your cash gifts and investments to make a portfolio that would give you some income. Today, however, your dividends and interest would do you more good being reinvested for the future and, if possible, taken out of your own taxable estate. You want to invest more on level 4 of the pyramid. Instead of looking for cash flow supplements, you want an incremental increase in the value of your investments with little or no taxable income.

Now is the time to meet with your financial advisor and plot a new course for your portfolio. Some of the revolving CDs you've owned that helped you pay for your home entertainment center or for new baby clothes every six weeks can now be liquidated in favor of longer-term investments. Growth stocks or growth-oriented mutual funds would be appropriate investments. If you feel comfortable with a little more risk, putting a small percentage of your capital into aggressive growth mutual funds specializing in emerging companies or in global funds investing in foreign securities could lead to a significant capital gain.

Owners of assets other than stock or money instruments should also review their holdings. Perhaps now is the time to have their collection reappraised and to replace their collection of minor paintings, sculpture, stamps, or other collectibles for one or two major acquisitions that stand a chance of gaining considerably in value.

STEP 3: KNOW WHERE YOUR MONEY GOES.

In the stage of life from twenty-five to forty-five, spending for single individuals or a childless two-income couple was fairly open-ended. As we pointed out, strict budgeting wasn't necessary because most often income was greater than cash outlays, and financial responsibilities were virtually nonexistent. In this stage of life, forty-five to sixty, the picture is quite different. Most people in this age group have several established responsibilities such as mortgages, payments on tax shelters, and life, car, and household insurance premiums. If they have children, they have the added medical, clothing, food, and educational expenses of their families. And of course there are still the long-term needs of retirement and, perhaps, caring for elderly parents. Because of all these demands on current income, even the highest-earning individuals in this group need a fairly detailed budget to make sure that all of their financial goals are being met.

How do you make sure that you're putting aside enough money to meet all of your needs? One general fund for savings often doesn't provide an answer because you really don't know what your position is in relationship to any one obligation. You'll have a clearer understanding of your goals if you set up separate accounts targeted for a variety of needs. Your most accessible account should be for household money. You'll want checking privileges linked to the account that could be opened at a savings bank, commercial bank, or brokerage firm.

You might want to have a separate money market account that is your discretionary fund—money you can use for shopping, travel, and entertainment. If you separate this from household money, emergency funds, and savings for future obligations, you're less likely to allow your discretionary spending to eat into funds targeted for other needs.

Of course, your emergency fund should be in a high-interest-bearing account. If you haven't updated it to reflect three months of your current expenses, now's the time to do it.

The rest of your income that you want to put aside for future needs should be divided and invested for each specific need. Your particular target funds will reflect your individual needs, but common examples would include:

Tuition booster: Your kids are approaching college age. The tuition is covered adequately by investments you made when they were just babies. However, things being as tough as they always are for emerging adults, you'd like a little nest egg for your kids to give them a foothold when they start out on their own, or to help pay for postgraduate education. Part of the money you've been putting away for tuition, you now put into shorter-term (e.g., five-year) instruments to build up a postgraduate fund.

Parent Fund: Your parents may have prepared themselves for retirement, but you're still concerned that long-term medical costs could limit their choices for living arrangements in their final years. To make sure that your parents can live as they want throughout their retirement years, you can make regular contributions into an emergency account for them. The investment you choose for the money will depend on your parents' health and financial situation. If the need for income is immediate, income-oriented stocks, Government National Mortgage Association or corporate bonds funds may be the best investment. If, however, your parents are secure for five or ten more years, you might opt to take advantage of the higher return on your money offered by investments such as bonds that mature in five or seven years.

Retirement Nest Egg: In your twenties and thirties, the maximum contribution to your IRA was about all you could manage to put toward your retirement. Now, however, you probably can allocate more money each year to your retirement. Look for the long-term investments that will give you the benefit of high return, the lower tax on capital gains, or even the tax-exempt status of municipal bonds. You can take some risk with this money, and that risk will give you the opportunity for greater returns on your investment. Growth stocks, convertible bonds, real estate income limited partnerships, growth-oriented mutual funds, and zero coupon tax-free bonds all would be good investments for your retirement target fund.

Your investment choices will be guided by the economic climate at the time. Are interest rates on bonds high? Zeros will lock in a high rate for you. Is the market booming? Growth stocks might be a good choice then. If you seem to be in a transition where interest rates are good but coming down and the market seems poised to take off, convertible bonds give you the opportunity to lock in a high interest rate and then trade in your bond for shares in the company if the stock becomes more valuable than the bond.

How much of your income should be allocated to each target fund? You'll have to use your own understanding of your financial needs or the advice of a financial counselor for the answer to that question. Common sense will prevail. If you don't have the money you need for college tuitions and your children are approaching college age, your tuition fund will get top priority. If your parents' health is failing and the rest of your needs are being met immediately, you may want to contribute as much as possible to their fund. And if your retirement funds look skimpy as you approach the age when you want to stop working, you'll need to divert as much money as possible to that fund. However, if the needs of the three funds are equal, investment opportunity might guide your allocation of funds. If, one year, an opportunity for a limited real estate partnership comes along that would be good for your future, you might want to cut back on your contributions to other target funds and buy shares in the partnership for your retirement fund. The following year you can give the money back to the other target funds.

Budgeting every dollar you earn so that it serves a purpose and helps you meet future goals takes some discipline and perseverance. However, the transition from a financial free spirit to a financial planner is critical to reaching economic maturity. It's the key to security for you and your family's present and future. Without it, the economic inconsistencies of the twenties and thirties become the financial uncertainties of middle and later life.

For Parents of Second Families: If you're reliving the early years of parenthood with a new son or daughter born in a second marriage, you know that mothering or fathering the second time around is just as exhausting—and exhilarating—as it was the first. Usually, it's not any easier for having had the same experience a decade ago.

The same is true of your economic responsibilities as a parent. Despite your age and experience, the steps for providing a secure future for your child are the same as they were when you were a young adult. You have to target specific amounts of money for the child's education right from the date of birth. And you will always need more money than you expected in order to buy diapers, clothes, pay medical expenses, and give your newest addition the same advantages you gave your first family.

Often, the beginning of a second family starts as the responsibilities for the first family are peaking—during high school and college years. You'll need not only to contribute to your baby's tuition fund, but to your adolescent's college fund as well. For parents with responsibilities to two families, this period may be even tighter financially than young adulthood. This is not to say that an austerity budget will be necessary. However, meticulous money management will be needed to make sure that your discretionary income doesn't just "disappear," and that your targeted income is not languishing in sluggish or deteriorating investments.

Common target funds for parents of second families would include:

New Tuition Fund: You should start to build up a tuition fund right after the birth of your child so that your money can work hardest for you in long-term investments. Zero coupon bonds maturing at dates corresponding to your child's four years at college are a convenient way to prepare for college costs.

Tuition Booster: You can get this fund going for your older children and your infant. Put the larger proportion of the money in short-term instruments for your older children. The smaller contributions to the infant's fund will grow to match those of his or her older siblings by the time he or she graduates from school.

Parent Fund: You may not have as much disposable income as you'd like to put into your parent fund. However, once your tuition fund for the new child is taken care of, you'll be able to divert part of that money to your parents' account.

Retirement Nest Egg: Beef up your IRA contributions if you haven't been putting in the maximum payment allowed. Then plan on allocating a larger part of your income than you normally would after your tuition and postgraduate funds are in place.

STEP 4: AVOID TAX SHOCK.

Your highest earning years are also your highest tax bill years. Between 35 and 50 percent of your income could be going to Uncle Sam unless you carefully plan your investment strategy to take advantage of tax-deductible and tax-deferred instruments and accounts. In the young adult years, you wanted to shelter income so that you had more to spend on setting up a home and lifestyle. In these midyears, however, the purpose behind your tax savings is different. You don't need the cash flow now. On the contrary, you need long-term gains that will provide you with funds for future commitments and retirement. And that should be the goal of your tax savings plan—to provide immediate tax deductions and long-term preservation and growth of principal. Thus, even if most of your investments have been in higher-risk instruments to improve your chances of short-term gain, you'll want to curb your gambling urges with these funds and invest in more moderate, conservative instruments such as those in level 4 in the investment pyramid.

Of course your first step in lowering taxes is to keep track of your deductible expenses. Next is to continue your annual contributions to an IRA or Keogh, if applicable. Maybe now you can make the maximum yearly contribution your goal every year. And don't forget to review your commitment to your company's retirement plan. Can you increase your annual contribution? If you do put more substantial sums into the company plan, will your cash flow needs still be adequately met? Most companies permit a change in contribution once a year.

If you weren't eligible to start a Keogh during your early professional years, that doesn't mean that you're not eligible now. Many professionals have sources of income outside their salaried jobs, such as speech-making, book-writing, or consulting services. If you have a secondary source of income, you may be eligible for a Keogh plan that would allow you to deduct another sizable part of your gross income as a contribution to this retirement plan.

Tax shelters, of course, provide another method for reducing your tax bill as well as providing long-term capital gains. At this stage in your financial life, you're probably in a good position to meet the one time periodic payments due on a shelter. One time payments in a public program may be as little as $5,000 and periodic payments on a private placement can range as high as $30,000 for four to five years.

Tax shelters are not the same type of investment as the retirement plans mentioned above. Most of you have probably read or heard about shelters that were disallowed or didn't provide the kind of benefits they were supposed to. Thus, while tax shelters can be a productive and effective part of your financial planning, you should approach this investment cautiously. Make sure that you buy into one that has been investigated by a trusted financial advisor—either your broker or your accountant—and that will still be viable under current tax legislation. You want to avoid those shelters that are poor business risks and may not provide you with a good future return. You also want to avoid shelters that are questionable and may be disallowed by the IRS.

Because you do have a sizable amount of cash you can use in tax-sheltered investments, you may be tempted to shelter almost all of your income. This is not a wise move for two reasons: First, the financial burden of such a large shelter investment might begin to outweigh the deduction benefits. You don't want to get in a situation where your expenses in the long run are greater than your tax savings. Second, if you shelter too much of your income, you're almost guaranteeing yourself an audit—a process even the most fastidious record keeper doesn't look forward to.

STEP 5: PLAN FOR SHORT-TERM AND LONG-TERM FINANCIAL NEEDS.

Future goals are the heart of financial planning for this age group. Short-term goals that you had during early adulthood mostly have been met. You have the car you wanted. You're comfortable in your main residence and perhaps in your vacation home. Basically, you've got the accouterments of the lifestyle you were trying to build in the previous stage of life, and your concerns have turned toward the future. For many people, the only short-term goal to meet is college tuition for the children. What you'll want to do now is beef up the funds you've been building since the children were infants. A few larger contributions to the tuition funds can provide a cushion if unexpected expenses arise or if postgraduate education becomes necessary.

Aside from tuition or possible medical expenses, short-term goals take a back seat to long-term investing for the future in this life stage. Plans for the future include building retirement reserves for yourself and, perhaps, for your parents if you feel that they will be unable to cover their living costs in later years. Most of the plans described in the last section of tax-advantaged investing are suitable for long-term financial planning. However, the only way that any of them will help you reach your goal of a comfortable retirement is with regular contribution habits. Your most important strategy for providing security for the future during these years is to treat your retirement plans as you do your mortgage commitments. If this kind of discipline is not your strong point, leave the contributions up to your employer or your broker: Make automatic payments out of your brokerage account or your paycheck.

What should your financial goal be for retirement? About 50 to 80 percent of your salary per year before retirement is what most people need. If you're used to a high income, you may want your whole salary replaced.

One way to estimate your retirement fund goals is to determine how much of your income you'll need to replace beyond your social security benefits. Currently, an employee earning about $16,000 can expect his or her social security benefits to replace about 40 percent of annual income. However, an employee earning close to the maximum amount of income covered by social security ($39,600 in 1985) can expect to have only about 28 percent of his or her income replaced by social security payments. The rest of the income would have to come out of pension plans and personal savings. Therefore, you'll want to construct a retirement savings plan that will replace the amount of income not covered by a company pension and social security benefits. Keep in mind that if you file a single return and your annual income exceeds $25,000, your social security payments will be subject to taxation. Couples filing jointly have a $32,000 income ceiling.

For example, let's say that you and your spouse want to replace 80 percent of your $40,000 income ($32,000) after retirement. Social security will replace 28 percent ($11,200) of your original income. Your personal retirement plan should cover the other $20,800 a year for your expected life span. If you and your spouse put a total of only $2,000 annually into an IRA from the time you are forty until the time you are sixty-five, you'll have more than enough money to secure your retirement income. Assuming that the money compounded at an interest rate of 10 percent during that time, you'd have salted away enough money to give you a maximum of $24,000 a year for twenty years of retirement.

If you meet the goals of the middle years, you'll be setting up the framework for a secure and comfortable retirement. Going into later life without financial worries is the ultimate goal of your investment strategies.

Ages 45–60: Goals
- Increase net worth.
    Invest in growth-oriented and tax-advantaged investments.
- Lower taxes through careful tax planning.
- Prepare for the future.
    Make regular contributions to target funds.

15
PROVIDING FOR ELDERLY PARENTS

The latter part of this stage in life often brings with it a confusing alteration in parent/child relationships. Your parents—even in adulthood—have been a source of shelter, food, and emotional stability. While they're alive, you're still someone's child. You may carry the burdens of a career, marriage, and parenthood, but at your parents' home you're still someone else's responsibility.

That relationship can change dramatically as you reach late middle age. Suddenly you discover that your mother hasn't done her wash in a month. She has forgotten. Upon further investigation, you realize that she hasn't cared for her house—always immaculate in the past—in weeks either. Your mother is no longer the anchor in your life that she was just last year. She needs you to take care of her, to become her parent for the last years of her life.

The transition from child to custodian is a difficult one. Sometimes it takes place over a period of years and the metamorphosis almost goes unnoticed until you realize that you're performing some specific act of caring that your mother always did for you. Sometimes, however, the transition can occur overnight, as in the case of a stroke or other health emergency.

Much of your care for your elderly parents will be in the form of making sure that their living circumstances are comfortable—that they have enough company, eat properly, and receive the right medical care. In the beginning, you might pick up the tab for the groceries, the doctor bill, or some other little expense. As time goes on and the costs begin to become substantial, however, you'll probably realize that you'll need a more formal financial arrangement.

AUGMENTING YOUR PARENTS' INCOME

If you begin to make significant contributions to your parents' income, you'd be wise to consider the tax implications of that cash flow and plan a strategy that will give you the greatest tax benefits while providing your parents with the greatest income.

On the most basic level, you can claim your parents as dependents if you are providing greater than 50 percent of their support. The IRS allows the standard $1,000 deduction (which may increase in the forthcoming tax code revisions) for children supporting parents whose income *outside of social security benefits* doesn't exceed $1,000 per year.

If your contribution to your parents' income is less than 50 percent of their support, you can still deduct your payment of grocery, utility, or medical payments from your income. Just make sure that you keep careful records of the bills you've paid and then itemize those expenses on your tax return.

Giving your parents money outright, however, is not always the most advantageous method of contributing to their support for you or for them. It increases the strain on your budget and often makes the parents feel like a burden—a position most elderly find uncomfortable. Instead, consider putting your contributions into investments that have good growth and/or income potential. These securities will compound the value of your support and offer secure income for your parents that doesn't come out of your family budget. Options for investment plans for parents include the following:

Whole Life Insurance Policies: Take out a policy on your parents that offers a cash value component. Your regular premium payments constitute your contribution to their support. When your parents need money, you can have the policy augment their income in two ways: (1) have the income thrown off by the investments of the cash value (e.g., bond interest or stock dividends) paid out to your parents; or (2) if a larger sum of money is needed, you could take out a low-interest loan against the policy, the principal of which doesn't need to be repaid regularly. In fact, if the principal isn't repaid at the time of the death of the insured, it is simply deducted from the death benefit. The death benefit in this case isn't the primary reason for the insurance. Instead, the purpose of the policy is to provide a source of income for your parents that doesn't strain your budget. Thus, a reduced death benefit isn't a major concern.

Custodian Account: Most people think of a custodian account for tuition funds for children. However, this type of account can be used for your parents as well. You can give up to $10,000 a year to each parent without incurring a gift tax. That money can be invested a number of ways to provide a steady source of income for your parents. Certificates of deposit or Treasury bills rolled over (i.e., investment is renewed) at maturity are secure instruments. Longer-term CDs, such as three- or five-year certificates, are available with a monthly interest payout option.

A brokerage account with income-producing and growth investments provides a more diverse approach. The slight increase in risk is offset by the chance for capital gains that may provide a greater income or greater principal amount for you as time goes by.

TAKING OVER

If your parents are particularly frail, housebound, or—in the case of a surviving parent—unfamiliar with financial management, you may want to take your role in their economic well-being one step farther and open a joint account with one parent. A joint account gives you and your parent equal access to and control over the money deposited in the account. You'd keep the account under your parent's social security number so that any income would not be added to your taxable estate. Your parents would still be able to direct their finances in the way that they want, but you would be able to cash checks for them, pay for cleaning and grocery bills, and make cash gifts easily into the account. One aspect of having a joint account with your parents that will have to be clarified before you approach the bank or brokerage firm is the right of survivorship of the joint account holders. Do your parents want the account balance to go to you automatically at their death, or do they want the money to be returned to their estate to be dispersed according to their wills? If the money is to be returned to the estate, you'll want to make sure that you and your parents sign an agreement to that effect and that the brokerage firm or bank will honor the arrangement.

A joint account is good for elderly parents who might be physically frail, but who still have their mental acuity. However, for parents who are mentally incapable of guiding their own affairs, you'll want to be given power of attorney over their estate at minimum. Power of attorney allows you to make financial decisions for your parents without asking for their consent for a given transaction. A lawyer usually draws up an agreement and issues a power that brokerages and banks honor. Often a brokerage firm has its own form, or power, that you simply sign and have notarized. A power of attorney may be used not only for cases where parents are mentally incompetent, but also can be issued for a particular time span, such as for the duration of a trip overseas or a hospital stay.

If the prognosis for your parent or parents is poor in the next few years and the assets are of any great amount, you probably will want to become the trustee of their estate. You would set up the trust with the help of a lawyer. Thereafter, as trustee, you would manage your parents' bills, taxes, and investments as if they were your own. Your parents would still file a tax return, though, and all income and deductions would be credited to their social security numbers.

If you're uncomfortable taking on total responsibility for your parents' estate, you may want to make the bank most familiar with your parents' finances co-trustee of the estate. However, you would be unwise to leave the estate completely in the bank's hands because a bank can never give your parents' finances the kind of individualized attention necessary for optimum management. Also, banks usually levy a substantial fee for their services as co-trustee. You might consider interviewing a few representatives from brokerage firms before turning to a bank. With the guidance of a broker, perhaps you would feel comfortable managing your parents' estate yourself and be able to avoid the costs of a bank co-trustee.

The arrangements you and your parents make for managing their estate in the event that they are incapable should be settled *in advance* of the need for the transfer of responsibility. Proving that your parents are mentally incompetent and unable to control their finances responsibly after the fact is a traumatizing, expensive, and often unsatisfactory way to gain control of their estate. Your ability to manage the funds in the way that you think is best (and even in the manner that your parents might have thought was best), may be compromised by the legal limits on your freedom as a court-appointed trustee or guardian of the estate. Only the most conservative investments may be allowed. Furthermore, you won't be allowed the flexibility to redirect your parents' assets in a manner that will fulfill their financial needs and obligations. Thus, even though discussing a future situation in which your parents may be mentally or physically disabled is difficult and painful, you need to steel yourself for the discussion in order to protect your parents and their assets in the future.

IF YOUR PARENTS SURVIVE YOU

Most of us draw up our wills with our children and grandchildren in mind. However, for this generation who may be providing for their elderly parents even as they enter retirement, a will has to straddle both the older and the younger generation.

For instance, if you are the trustee of your parents' estate, you should arrange to pass that responsibility on to someone equally qualified and trustworthy to manage your parents' finances and cover necessary living and medical expenses. If you own an insurance policy on your parents that is providing them with regular income, make sure that your estate continues to provide regular premium payments for the policy. In other words, make sure that your estate is arranged to continue whatever kind of support you were providing for your parents while you were alive.

Financial aid to elderly parents is an issue very much on all of our minds. You want to make sure that your parents don't suffer in their last years, that you give them the comfort and support they gave you. At the same time, you know that your income may be limited just when your parents need your help. The only way around this economic conflict is with planning. Take a part of your retirement fund and target it as an emergency fund for your parents. Invest some of the money in long-term instruments that may provide regular income if it is needed. Another part of the fund can be invested in growth products that will make your contributions grow in worth as your parents reach an age when they need the funds. By planning now, you can avoid a painful economic crisis later in life when you aren't able to afford to help your parents in the way you would want to.

Options for Augmenting Your Parents' Income
- **Out-of-pocket support**
    - Tax-deductible expense
    - Possible additional "dependent" deduction
- **Custodial**
    - Targeted fund for parents
    - Money taxed at parents' lower rate
- **Whole life policy**
    - Cash value investments pay parents directly
    - Inexpensive loans against cash value available

16
REVIEWING YOUR INSURANCE NEEDS

Your insurance needs in the first life stage probably grew from minimal to elaborate as you acquired a house, two cars, got married, had children, and perhaps even bought a vacation home. In the second stage of life, the nature of your insurance needs will change dramatically again. Much of the insurance you have today may be unnecessary once the children are grown, your house is paid for, and retirement approaches. However, other insurance needs, such as for medical catastrophe, may be of interest as you enter your later years. As was mentioned earlier, a quick periodic review of your insurance policies every few years or after a major life event will help you determine how you should invest in life insurance.

TERM VERSUS LIFE INSURANCE

Your father probably told you that after a certain age, whole life insurance was a better investment than term. However, with life insurance being a fairly standard corporate benefit, individual needs for whole life insurance aren't what they used to be. If you do have a benefit of life insurance through your company, or if you can purchase insurance inexpensively through your employer, you may only want to augment that benefit with term insurance when your living expenses take a sudden, temporary jump. For instance, you might want extra insurance when your children are in college and their tuition adds a large sum to your annual overhead. Then, if something were to happen to you, your extra term insurance would cover the additional costs of college education.

For those of you whose company has no insurance benefit that is suitable for you, whole life insurance is probably the most economical choice during these years. In the early first stage, term would have been a suitable, less expensive alternative to whole life. However, as you get older, term insurance becomes increasingly more expensive while giving you no cash surrender value in return. You only receive a death benefit. During these more lucrative years, you can afford whole life insurance that will earn you tax-free dividends or interest on the cash value of your policy while it protects you.

As mentioned in an earlier chapter on insurance, many different varieties of whole life insurance (e.g., variable and universal) are offered currently. What type of whole life you choose will depend on your financial needs for the present and future.

FOR SECOND FAMILIES

Parents of second families will find that their insurance needs are increasing rather than decreasing in this stage of life. You'll want to add insurance specifically for the new members of the family. The amount of the coverage will vary with your new family's needs. If you are assuming responsibility for a college-age adolescent as well as a newborn, you'll want your policy to be able to cover the tuition costs and the financial burdens of raising the younger child.

A term policy taken out to boost your existing coverage is probably the most economical way of providing for your second family. You'll want to specify that your new partner and child or children are the beneficiaries of the extra policy so that the death benefits go to the individuals for whom they were intended. In this manner, you can be sure that your first family receives the benefits you originally planned for them and your new family has a separate policy protecting them also.

INSURANCE FOR THE UNINSURABLE

If you are an older parent with a new family, you may find that your health profile raises eyebrows at most life insurance companies and prevents you from getting the kind of coverage you think you need. If you find yourself in that position, you have a couple of options for insuring yourself:

Ask another family member, such as a younger spouse, to take out a policy on you and make him- or herself the beneficiary.

Look into insurance coverage designed specifically for individuals with health conditions that make them undesirable to most insurance carriers. Such insurance is called "rated" insurance. You won't get as much coverage for your dollar as you would in an ordinary policy, but for the extra money, you'll have peace of mind.

USING INSURANCE AS AN INVESTMENT VEHICLE

The investment angle of whole life insurance offers the policy holder a number of interesting alternatives for meeting financial obligations in his or her present life while protecting the family against unforeseen disasters.

Tax-Sheltered Tuition and Starter Fund: You can structure the investment of the cash value of your policy to pay out interest to your child in college every year as well as to subsidize his or her income during the few first years as an independent adult. The benefits of using your insurance in this manner is that, as the owner of the policy, you control the accumulated income of your policy until death. No time limits apply such as would on UGMAs. There are only two drawbacks on this kind of arrangement: You will be paying interest charges on the money borrowed against your policy; and under the proposed revision of the tax laws, loans totaling more than $50,000 taken against an insurance policy could be taxed as regular income, and interest payments on policy loans might not be deductible. Thus, before you set up this kind of a financial arrangement, weigh the benefits against the drawbacks to make sure that in the end it will be a financially wise strategy.

An Asset for You and Your Elderly Parents: An insurance policy can provide an emergency fund or regular income for elderly, disabled parents and at the same time provide a future asset for you. In this situation, you buy a policy covering your parents naming yourself as the beneficiary. As the owner of the policy, you are responsible for premium payments and also have control over the cash value. If your parents need regular income, you can send them the interest or dividends thrown off by the investments made with the cash value of the policy. If you suddenly need a large sum of money for medical or other payments, you can borrow against the value of the policy. Because you are the beneficiary of the policy, any death benefits from the policy (minus outstanding loans) will be left to you.

Investment Fund: The income earned on the cash value of your insurance policy compounds annually. Though the actual cash payout of the policy will go to your beneficiary, low interest rate loans against the cash value are available. Thus, by building up your cash value, you're building up an inexpensive source of cash for your use now.

Insurance needs are hard to predict throughout a life stage because they will be altered at every crossroad in your life. To help you feel confident that you're adequately insured and that you're using insurance to its best advantage in your situation, you'll want the same trusted relationship with your insurance broker that you have with your financial advisor. He or she should not only help you purchase the necessary coverage for yourself, your family, and your belongings over the course of your life, but should also advise you on ways to make your policy work for you while you're investing your money in it.

WHEN YOU'RE THE BENEFICIARY

During the second stage of your financial life you may find yourself the recipient of death benefits from an insurance policy on a close relative. The events surrounding the receipt of the proceeds from an insurance policy can make a normally sound investor behave irresponsibly. Once the emotional trauma of the death has passed, however, the recipient of the death benefits regrets having acted unwisely or in haste.

Try to remember that the insured planned to give the money to you before death as a way to help you reach your goals or to provide you with security. At first the money may seem like a cheap payoff for the loss of a loved one, but once your grief is resolved, you may see the death benefits as a way to build a living memory of the insured. Maybe it could pay for your child's education, decrease a loan, or provide for a much needed additional room onto the house.

However you might choose to use the money in the future, the important step for the present is to put the money in a secure short-term investment where it can earn interest safely while you decide how you eventually want to invest the funds. A six-month certificate of deposit or a Treasury bill would be good transitional investments for this kind of inheritance.

Insurance Review:
- Review your insurance needs at every major life change.
- Consider whole life insurance in light of its investment value.
- Use additional term insurance to augment a whole life policy or employee insurance benefit.
- Set aside inherited insurance proceeds in a short-term secure investment until you're past the initial shock of the death.

17

REVIEWING YOUR RETIREMENT PLANS

Suddenly, retirement doesn't loom in the distance. At the end of this second life stage you may be within five years of retirement. As a result of the long-term planning you've followed throughout this life stage, you've met your financial goal for the years ahead. Now, however, you need to reorganize your investments so that they provide a regular, sufficient income that is as free from tax burdens as possible, that will continue for the remainder of your life, and that is flexible enough to provide emergency funds for unexpected medical or other costs.

The financial strategy for your retirement years should be planned to reach the same basic goals you had during your wage earning years. You want to maximize your liquidity by protecting your income from excessive taxation and by earning high returns on your money. You also want to enjoy life today while making sure that you have security for tomorrow. The following seven guidelines to financial preparation for retirement can help you attain these goals:

Estimate Annual Income Needs.

You've been trying to estimate your retirement income needs using formulas and other calculations, but now that you're within a few years of retirement, you probably have a much clearer and more realistic idea of what you want to do after you leave the office and how much it is going to cost you. To make a complete record of your estimated needs, draw up a new personal financial review that reflects your projected living expenses during retirement. Also remember gifts that you may want to make to children and grandchildren as well as contributions to nonprofit organizations. When you arrive at a monthly expense sum, multiply it by 12 and you have your annual income estimate.

Reorganize Your Portfolio.

Now that you know what your cash flow needs are, sit down with your various retirement plan portfolios as well as with your projections for social security income, distributions from profit sharing, and deferred compensations plan funds. Your objective is to plan a strategy of investment that will provide you with income without eroding your principal or incurring large tax bills.

First estimate your social security benefits. The following chart will help you.

Subtract that figure from your projected expenses for the month. Also, if you have a pension coming to you, subtract your monthly payments from your expenses also. The rest of your income will have to be covered by your savings and retirement plans.

When planning your cash flow, make sure you keep the following guidelines in mind:

Watch Out for Social Security Taxation.

If you're planning to have a joint adjusted gross income (after deductions, and including *half* of your social security benefits and

ESTIMATING YOUR BENEFITS

Approximate monthly retirement benefits, in today's dollars, for a worker retiring at age 65.

YOUR AGE In 1985	$10,000	$16,000	$23,000	$31,000	$40,000+
		YOUR PRESENT ANNUAL EARNINGS			
65	$383	$522	$665	$698	$717
64	392	533	679	716	737
63	398	541	691	730	754
62	403	547	698	741	767
61	404	548	701	744	773
56–60	406	552	705	753	789
51–55	410	558	712	771	820
46–50	414	565	720	793	858
41–45	395*	540*	685*	768*	844*
31–40	396*	543*	683*	775*	869*
Under 31	386*	530*	663*	753*	850*

The table assumes steady employment and average pay increases.

* These amounts have been reduced for early retirement at age 65; the "normal" retirement age is higher for these workers.

Source: *Wall Street Journal*, 30 April 1985; originally from William M. Mercer-Meidinger Inc.

any tax-exempt income) of over $32,000, or a single adjusted gross income of over $25,000 per year, your social security will be taxed. The tax cannot amount to more than half of your benefit, but that limit offers little consolation.

Minimize Your Adjusted Gross Income.

What can you do to avoid a stiff tax bill while keeping up the lifestyle you planned? Make sure you take advantage of any tax deductions available to you that will bring down your gross income. You might consider remortgaging the house, for instance, if your payments are now mostly principal at this point. You can use the mortgage money to invest in higher-yielding vehicles than the money that will provide you with regular income. At the same time, you'll be increasing your deductions by taking on the high interest payments of a new mortgage.

Another tax deduction that many retirees forget is the annual IRA and/or Keogh contribution. You can continue to contribute to both of these accounts and deduct your payment until you're 70.5 years of age.

Limit Taxable Income.

Try to make as much of your income tax exempt as possible so that you're taxed only on your social security income. One way to accomplish this is to take advantage of long-term tax-free municipal bonds (bought from your state of residence so as to be triple tax-free) and state-tax-free government agency or treasury bonds. When your zero coupons or other bonds bought for your retirement mature, roll the money over into tax-free bonds that will provide you with steady income for twenty or twenty-five years.

Plan for the Future.

Take advantage of long-term securities that have a high rate of return. Too often, people approaching retirement feel that only short-term investments are prudent for their golden years which, they believe, might be cut short at any moment. They fear that long-term investments might tie up their money so that it's not available in an emergency. Both of these beliefs are misconceptions today. First of all, most retirements last fifteen or more years. You don't want to plan a cash flow for fifteen years only to find at age eighty that you feel terrific but are penniless. Long-term investments, such as municipal bonds, preserve your principal while paying out a regular income. Other investment alternatives, such as zero coupon bonds, allow a small principal investment to grow sizably over the life of the security so that you have a source of income in your later years as you need it. However you arrange your cash flow for retirement years, you should always plan for your source of income to outlive you.

Second, high-quality bonds usually don't lose much of their face value. You almost always can sell them in an emergency and count on getting all or nearly all of your principal back in as little as five to seven days.

Use Your IRA/Keogh Account Wisely.

The government says that you are allowed to start taking money out of your IRA or Keogh account when you are 59.5, but you don't *have* to start taking any payments out until you are 70.5, and you may continue contributing until you are age 70. Payments from IRA and Keogh accounts are taxed as regular income, so you want to postpone using those funds until your income is at its lowest level.

Once you start withdrawing money from the fund, keep in mind that a new law allows the minimum amount you must take out (the amount of the account divided by your life expectancy) to be recalculated every year. Such recalculation can stretch your retirement fund considerably. For instance, under the old law, if you were a woman starting to withdraw funds at age seventy, you'd have to take out $1/15$ of your fund every year because your life expectancy would be fifteen years. Thus, if you lived past age eighty-five, you'd have already depleted your retirement account.

Under the new law, you'd take out $1/15$ of your funds at age seventy also. However, at age seventy-five, your life expectancy would be 12.1 years, so you could reduce the amount of money you withdraw to $1/12$ of the remaining funds. The chart below will help you envision how this recalculation can reduce the minimum withdrawals over a period of thirty years and make your retirement fund a steady source of income throughout your retirement.

CALCULATING MINIMUM IRA WITHDRAWALS		
AT AGE: MEN	WOMEN	DIVIDE ACCOUNT BALANCE BY:
65	70	15.0
70	75	12.1
75	80	9.6
80	85	7.5
85	90	5.7
90	95	4.2
95	100	3.1

Note: Other figures are used for joint life expectancy.

Source: *Wall Street Journal*, 11 September 1985, originally from Internal Revenue Service

Divest Your Assets.

Over the years, you've built up your assets in a number of ways. Much of that building was probably done by consolidating smaller investments into larger, more profitable ones. However, during the latter part of this life stage, you're going to take the reverse strategy—breaking down large investments into smaller ones to help you maintain a regular cash flow. Instead of one large, long-term bond, for instance, you may buy several smaller ones that mature on staggered dates, thereby providing you with income for a number of years at various interest rates. You also would want to cash out (withdraw the cash value of) your whole life insurance policies, provided that you have no dependents, and use that money to seek a higher rate of return.

Another part of your divestment as you near retirement might concern valuables that you've collected. If you intend to bequeath a certain cherished collection, painting, or piece of jewelry to someone or to a charity, perhaps you should plan to make your bequest during your retirement rather than in your will. By giving away your property while you're alive, you can make sure that your valuables go to the right person and are cared for in the way you would want them to be.

Divestment also can take place by means of annual gifts of money that you intend to go to family members. Depending on your tax status, you may benefit from making your cash gifts out of your estate during retirement rather than in your will.

Review Your Will.

In your earlier years, the focus of your financial planning was on insuring and protecting present and future income. However, as you near retirement and your current obligations are under control, protecting your assets after your death becomes an equally important aspect of economic planning. You want to make sure that your carefully planned estate is inherited as you want it to be.

You probably have a will that you've looked over once or twice since it was drawn up decades ago. Your intentions might be the same now as they were then, but the tax laws that will affect your estate most likely have changed. Therefore, a complete review of your estate is necessary when you retire.

You also should go through your assets with your accountant or a tax lawyer to make sure that your estate is structured in such a way as to take advantage of whatever estate tax exemptions are available. As mentioned before, the current marital deduction allows a spouse to inherit virtually any amount from a deceased partner without paying tax. However, by taking advantage of the marriage deduction, the surviving spouse may pay less in taxes, but the family inheriting the estate after his or her death might pay more in tax because they'll be able to take advantage of only one $500,000–600,000 estate tax exemption for the property listed under the surviving partner's name. Instead, if the assets were kept in both spouses' individual names, the family could take the $500,000–600,000 estate tax exemption for assets listed under each spouse's name, thus doubling the exemption.

For example, couple A and B have assets worth $1,000,000. When A has a heart attack, he and B review all of their assets and separate their joint holdings so that all of their assets are divided equally between them. When A dies several years later, B inherits all of A's $500,000 worth of assets tax free. Now her total estate is worth $1,000,000 of which only $500,000 will be exempt from estate tax. The $500,000 she inherited tax free from A will now be taxable at the regular graduated estate tax rate.

If A and B had managed the estate in another manner, however, the whole $1,000,000 could have passed to their family federal tax free. If A's $500,000 estate, the whole of which is tax-exempt, had been put into a trust (according to specified legal conditions) at the time of his death rather than transferred to his wife's estate, it would have passed directly to the family without being taxed because it had remained part of A's tax-exempt estate rather than being combined into B's estate. B could still benefit from the estate if this type of trust were structured to pay her income for the duration of her life. Then, B's estate, worth only $500,000 would also fall under the federal government's estate tax exemption limit, so the family would eventually inherit the whole $1,000,000 federal estate tax free in this plan.

Insure Your Family Against Estate Tax.

If, despite good planning, your family is likely to end up with a sizable estate tax (up to 50 percent of the amount above $500,000–600,000), you'll want to insure that the tax doesn't create a financial burden for your beneficiaries. Remember, Uncle Sam expects full payment in ninety days, and that might not be enough time for your family to sort out your estate and develop a financial strategy for the inheritance.

To provide available funds for estate tax, consider purchasing life insurance policies for you and your partner, the death benefit of which would cover the estate taxes estimated to be due to the

UNLIMITED MARRIAGE DEDUCTION

CURRENT ASSETS	ASSETS AFTER DEATH OF "A"	TAX STATUS OF ESTATE AFTER DEATH OF "B"
A = $500,000 B = $500,000	B = $500,000 + 500,000 (A)* $1,000,000	B = $1,000,000 − 500,000† $ 500,000 (taxable)

MAXIMUM ESTATE TAX EXEMPTION

A = $500,000 B = $500,000	B = $500,000 (A = $500,000 (in trust)	B = $500,000 − 500,000† + 0 A = $500,000 (in trust) − 500,000† 0 $0 taxable

* Totally tax-deductible
† Tax-exempt

government. If you or your partner are uninsurable, suggest that someone in your family purchase the insurance policy and reimburse him or her for the payments.

These seven steps will help you prepare for a financially secure retirement as well as insure that your estate is managed properly after your death, but they don't prepare you for making the difficult decisions about retiring from work.

To Work or Not to Work.

You've probably been planning your retirement as a time when your tax level will be lower enabling you to draw on your retirement funds without paying half of your income to Uncle Sam. The day you get your gold watch, however, you also may get several calls from firms asking for you to work as a consultant. The work sounds interesting, you can set your own hours, and the fee you'll be paid is very handsome. Therein, however, lies your problem. The income actually could come close to what you were earning on the job if you take on the clients who have already written to you. Making that kind of money, you'd be certain to lose a good chunk of your social security check because, at the time of this writing, earnings above $5400–7320 effect a reduction in social security benefits. Your check would be further reduced by taxes if your earnings topped the current $25,000–32,000 income level above which social security benefits are taxed. How can you continue to be productive without losing much of the retirement benefits you've worked so hard to secure?

If you don't want to worry about taxes, you could keep your income below the maximums set by the government. Combining volunteer work with a modest amount of income-producing work is one way to reduce your income. If you want a higher income, however, you won't be able to avoid paying taxes altogether. Tax bills will be as much a part of your financial responsibility after retirement as they were before, and minimizing those bills will be as much a part of your financial strategy as it was before. The following rules of thumb will help you avoid high tax bills:

Continue Your IRA/Keogh Contributions: When you retire, you'll most likely be at an age when you not only can withdraw from your retirement accounts, but you can also continue to contribute to them as well. If you don't need to use the funds, you might consider just keeping up your regular contributions and holding out on any withdrawals until your income is scaled back farther. Remember, however, that you *must* start withdrawing funds from these accounts at age 70.5.

Invest in Tax-Free Instruments: If your taxable income is going to be substantial even when you are required to withdraw funds from your IRA or Keogh account, start reorganizing your investments so that the income thrown off by them is tax-free.

Make a Gift: You can use either part of your income or money you must withdraw from your retirement funds to give cash gifts to your family that you might have left to them in your will. The money then is out of your taxable estate.

As you can see, your financial books are never really closed. Even after you've stopped earning outside income, you need to manipulate your portfolio to take advantage of changing economic climates and new investment opportunities. Similarly, you have to be on the alert for changes in the tax laws that may increase or decrease the income you've established for yourself in retirement.

Preparing for Retirement:
- **Know what your living expenses will be.**
- **Arrange for a secure income.**
- **Don't be shortsighted; plan for your later retirement too.**
- **Keep up your tax-avoidance strategies.**
- **Consider divesting part of your estate during your retirement years.**

Conclusion

I hope that you're now convinced that thinking about money is a profitable exercise, both financially and personally. It's your money; plan, use, and keep it wisely.

Successful investing and prosperous money management does not take undue time or undue amounts of money. What it does take, however, is a continuous and ongoing examination of your financial state of affairs. Each life cycle has its own money demands. By a careful match-up between these needs and the cash you have available, you can accomplish your own personal investment goals.

Financial plans obviously must be adapted and modified but if you are consistent in your approach and have the patience for these goals to be realized, your planning will be successful. Remember that just as there is no one universally correct investment goal, neither is there one right investment vehicle to meet that goal. Be aware of your own money and temperament, and concentrate on your own money needs.

CONCLUSION

As I stated from the first, it is never too late to begin your own lifetime investment program. The Five Steps to money management remain the same throughout all your financial life cycles. Even though your input will change, the format remains the same. Your financial today and tomorrow is within your own control. You now know how to use that control. Use it well.

—Barbara Lee

About the Authors

BARBARA LEE is a Senior Vice President/Financial Consultant with Shearson Lehman Brothers, Inc. She moved from New York City three years ago to open the Shearson office in Great Barrington, Massachusetts.

She is a graduate of Wellesley College and has been a stockbroker for ten years. She is also a magazine columnist and a radio commentator on business affairs. In 1984–85 she was used by *Fortune* magazine in their national advertising campaign. She lectures often to professional groups about money management.

PAULA M. SIEGEL divides her time between New York City and East Quogue, Long Island. She is a graduate of the S. I. Newhouse School of Journalism at Syracuse University and has been a freelance writer for eleven years. She writes frequently for many national magazines and has had two books published.